salmonpoetry

Diverse Voices from Ireland and the World

Also by John Morgan

Poems

THE BORDER WARS
THE BONE-DUSTER
THE ARCTIC HERD
THE INSIDE PASSAGE
THE CYCLIST
WALKING PAST MIDNIGHT
SPELLS AND AUGURIES
SPEAR-FISHING ON THE CHATANIKA: New and Selected Poems
RIVER OF LIGHT: A CONVERSATION WITH KABIR
ARCHIVES OF THE AIR
· THE MOVING OUT: Collected Early Poems

Essays

FORMS OF FEELING: POETRY IN OUR LIVES

The Hungers
of the World
New & Collected
Later Poems

JOHN MORGAN

Published in 2023 by

Salmon Poetry

Cliffs of Moher, County Clare, Ireland

Website: www.salmonpoetry.com

Email: info@salmonpoetry.com

ISBN 978-1-915022-33-2

Cover & Title Page Image: *"Tanana River Vista" a painting by Alaskan artist David Mollett*
Cover Design & Typesetting: *Siobhán Hutson*

Printed in Ireland by Sprint Print

Salmon Poetry gratefully acknowledges the support of
The Arts Council / An Chomhairle Ealaíon

for Nancy, Carla, Jeffrey, Ben, and Stella

Acknowledgements

Some of these poems were first published in the following magazines and anthologies: *The Alaska Quarterly Review, Ascent, bosque, Cape Discovery, Clover, Cirque, The Colorado Review, Crab Orchard Review, The Ekphrastic Review, Even the Daybreak—35 Years of Salmon Poetry, Field, Great River Review, Ice-Floe, In Like Company, The Kenyon Review, Mānoa, Marrow, Mercy of Tides* (Saltmarsh Pottery Press), *The North American Review, The Northern Review, Poetry Northwest, Porch, Prairie Schooner, The Quarterly Review of Literature Fiftieth Anniversary Anthology, Rapier, Rattle, Salt River Review, Shankpainter, The Southern Review, Subtropics, Verse-Virtual,* and *Words and Pictures.*

Spear-Fishing on the Chatanika: New and Selected Poems and *Archives of the Air* were originally published by Salmon Poetry. *River of Light: A Conversation with Kabir* was originally published by The University of Alaska Press and is reprinted with permission from the press.

I wish to thank The Alaska State Council on the Arts, The Rasmuson Foundation, and The Fine Arts Work Center for their generous support. Also my continuing gratitude to these friends for their helpful comments and suggestions over the years: Jean Anderson, Christianne Balk, Derick Burleson, Marjorie Cole, Burns Cooper, Joseph Enzweiler, Susheila Khera, John Kooistra, Cynthia Hardy, John Reinhard, Linda Schandelmeier, and Peggy Schumaker. And special thanks to Jessie Lendennie of Salmon Poetry for her very generous support and to Siobhán Hutson for her designs.

A NOTE ON THE ZUIHITSU

We tend to think of Japanese poems as tight, syllable counting, and focused on nature, but the zuihitsu is a kind of anti-haiku—a long, random prose piece, often numbered, that can bring up personal issues and include the social world. It's a form that allows for—even demands—free association. It can include quotations, sections in verse, confessional passages, philosophical ruminations, and whatever else comes to mind.

Contents

New Poems

from *Spear-Fishing on the Chatanika*

Archives of the Air

I

II.

ANALECTS (a gathering of literary fragments)

III.

Two Long Poems

New Poems

STRAY THOUGHTS ON AGING

Fairbanks, Alaska

Is everything new about getting old? Spring
and the melting snow, friends dropping away—
they sift underground, or washed by the wind
they circle the earth. Their names like chalk on
a blackboard pose the daunting equation of loss.

Yesterday I biked past the old beer and gun club,
rechristened "Hogwarts," to the edge of the slough
where it joins the big river. No bridge for miles
but a flagpole with pennants to summon
a boat when somebody needs to cross.

These blustery afternoons, deceptive in their
beauty—bright hopes leading us on. Fish camp
and then a hundred empty miles to the range
where mountains like grandparents lounging
on hammocks span the horizon. Clouds

like winged lions—Assyrian. Is heaven open
for business on days like this? And cycling back,
a bull moose browsing the roadside willows
turns his head and stares. He's like that difficult cousin
you can't help liking despite his prickly ways.

Brain circuits, axon and synapse, maybe
we've got it all wrong, like those late night
sophomore sessions when a light went on
and suddenly everything changed. Are we
our physical bodies? Are we anything else?

If the body's a river distilling the years,
then a time-lapse camera could track this life,
recording the snowballing wisps of decay, sloughed

skin and hair, like mayflies flitting, having their day,
while the waistline spreads like a delta toward the sea.

It leaves a glow, a whisper, a caress. Remember
that dusty floor we slept on before we owned
a bed? "But why do they call it sleeping?" you said.
Still there's a pungence to this breeze, a whiff of bliss.
Is heaven open for business on days like this?

NEXT TIME...

perhaps I'll become a stone
lying half sunk in a stream
waiting for the water to rise.
It's not easy to stay so still
and hold your mineral breath
while overhead the birds
paddle about the sky; not easy
to wait for the leaves to brown
and drop while the ducks row past
with their latest dutiful brood,
and salmon tickle your sides
as they churn upstream; to count
the minutes, hours, days until
islets of ice drift by,
and not to blink your crystalline eyes
when the whiteness spatters down.

Sometimes a fox glides past.
A cheerful cloud may wink.
A poet sits on a log and scatters
lines on a page. He thinks
he can capture your thoughts
but his verses put you to sleep
where you dream of
your former life as a lighthouse
scanning the patterned waves
for whales as they breach.

CONFESSIONAL

As saints look down from high glass walls
my Irish nursemaid Lily comes from behind
the curtain, and I ask her about her session
but she says that she can't tell me
since it's just between her and God.

So while she kneels and says her Hails
I mill around the empty church and find
a baby Jesus with every part of him
showing. He stands on a stone column
which tells how important he is

to the people who come here like Lily
to confess, light candles, and mumble
their requests to God and his mother Mary too.
But we don't believe that crap, my brother
told me, *since we're Jewish*, though what we do

believe I'm not quite sure. A metal bowl
sits at Jesus's feet and in the bowl are nickels,
dimes, and quarters. But one coin is much bigger
than the rest and bright and new. It's heavy
in my hand and has a bell on it plus words

that I can't read yet. It must be worth
a bundle so I'm thinking I could
stick it in my pocket, which I know
that would be wrong, but maybe I could
hide it in my closet or the sock drawer.

"What are you doing?" Lily says behind me.
"*Johnny, put that back!*" Shame wets
my cheeks and salt tears dribble to my lips.
I feel so bad that Lily who I love
is mad at me. But then she picks me up

and hugs me, so I know that she still
loves me and as she puts me in my stroller
it comes to me that one day when I'm older
I could join her church and have confession
since now I have a sin I could confess.

THE SINNER AT SIX

Into the candled dark where haloed strangers
mingled in jigsaw-puzzle windows, Lily,
my Irish nursemaid and first love, snuck me
whenever my Jewish parents nodded.
Back when the Mass was still in Latin,
one Sunday in my boredom
I begged to hold the string of holy beads
she counted on for luck and in
my fidgets twisted it until it broke
apart and spilled its tiny white
and purple jewels into my lap.

Shame wet my cheeks and terror
seized me by the throat. I knew
that I was damned and, worse, Lily
might also go to hell for what I'd done—,
and hell was like the front yard leaves we heaped
each fall and lit, each leaf a separate soul
that shriveled curling inward as it flamed,
then turned to smoke and ash. In hell, they said,
you burned like that forever. But seeing
my stricken face, she asked me why,
and when I unpeeled my young fists full
of tiny lights, she brushed my tears away,
and whispered that her beads could be restrung.

OLD JEWISH QUARTER, PRAGUE

"Morgenstern, Abraham I.VII.1869 Jana…"

The names in red hand-printed on beige walls
precede their dates (as known) in blocked
black ink, a tabernacle of the disappeared,
our family name among the thousands here.
Transported to the camps, they turned to ash
and blew away.
                    Outside, ancestral
gravestones scoured by age—a multitude
of slabs that pitch at angles and collapse.
Layered in dirt, the bones long since decayed,
hooded in moss, and Hebrew letters worn.
We join a line of patience passing by
to view a past we all are moving toward.
Does death erase the insults that they bore
whose lives are stitched in satin on the sky?

SABINA SPIELREIN, A LIFE

b. Rostov on Don, 1885

My father was a brutal man though kind
who, angry, thumped me on my bare behind
and swore he loved me. So I learned that love
means pain. And later when my monthly
blood began, I dreamed of ravishings by
clawed and wingéd monsters born from men.

A little sister's death undid my mind.
That's when the blows of lightning struck
and thundered in my head. My feet on fire
couldn't touch the ground. In bed for fortnights
at a time, I screamed my fury at the maid,
my mother, brothers, father, doctors.

I was not culpable for what I said.
They sent me to Geneva to get cured.
My healer was a charming man named Jung.
He let me have my say. Within two
months I'd talked the pains away. We sailed
the lake and held each other's hand.

He found a private spot to paddle me.
I called our sacred passion "poetry."
Seeking his art, I read his teacher's books
and analyzed my dreams. Jung took my
insights, mixed them with his own, and
published them. And then he broke my heart.

A hawk with eyes that frame and magnify
the sedge's tiny seeds, he hovers
over the Alpine meadow of my dream.
His curling talons suddenly extend.
He snakes his neck around, then dives
and rends the tangled longings in my breast.

I wrote to Freud, his master, to complain.
He said to let it go. I traveled to Vienna,
joined the inner band. My thoughts were
duly noted with my name. Ah, those
were the years of honey and sweet dust,
of operas, pastries, paintings, droll parades.

But then my family found a match and
drummed me home. I married a believer
in the book, a dour man. We had two
daughters and I probed their infants ways.
But when I passed my findings on
another man took credit once again.

The end was brutal—please don't avert your eyes.
A German SS unit bused us to the woods
outside of Rostov, stripped us, lined us up
beside a ditch. My daughters too. That death
is one of mankind's basic drives, I'd pointed
out to Freud. Hence war's bright thrill. Our bones
are mingled there. You can't tell which from which.

PATRIMONY

When he came home from the war
with a damaged ear, his voice
was still strong and sweet,
but, frowned on by my mother,
he rarely sang. It was a difficult marriage
an uncle once remarked, my mother's sarcasm
answered too often with blows.
And the boys it produced
were like bullets that fly off
in random directions and miss their marks.

But he drove me to see the bones
in the wide caverns of knowing—
the skulls with three horns,
backbones with spikes
restored, bones that sang of their lives
on prairies, in jungles and under the sea.

I loved those fossils almost as much as words,
which led to a dream of completion
that still escapes me. I look back
past the years of quarrels and bruisings,
to a time when hidden in a corner
by the back stairs,
alone with the booming world,
I could hear him sing in the shower
and learned something I needed to know.

IN SPIDER COUNTRY

In a breeze the web expands and sways, its guys
thread to the porch post and a bench where no one's
sat for days. The golden speckled spider's tiny
for this grand elaboration of trap. Does she

even remember that she shaped it? Does
she enjoy the breeze or worry it may tear
apart her lattice? Now her job is repair,
heavy maintenance, not creation—hurry

as the wind picks up and gaps appear a fly
could buzz right through. Two hungers drive her, food
and another which is pulsing in her nerves—a spider's
mothering thought. Where is that many-legged mate?

Rain at night. Next day, the web in tatters and
no sign of her. I hope she's found a safer
place to weave. But as I lean in for a closer
look, a silken thread attaches to my cheek.

NORTHWEST SHREW-MOLE

On its back on the lawn, black dots
for eyes, this rigid palm-sized
package, brown fur, pink snout,
with its teeth in a sweet
bucktooth grin, where a couple of flies
have begun their interrogations. No ants
yet or crows, as if it might soon
come to, and return to its
underworld works, the cavern
of roots, slugs and worms,
a humid dream-space of heavy labor
that circles below our middle kingdom.

*

That night, swollen, sullen, stiff,
I stare at the spackled swirls
of ceiling constellations, the grit
of my past washed off, my thoughts
like a broom handle, reaching
toward that one strand of web
to sweep it away as the coming peace
folds over me...when a tiny annoyance,
a distant train-horn, dribble of rain,
pulls me back into time, returning me
to the joy not yet over of days, years,
a wind-chime, a rainbow, a shrew-mole...

*

A recent demise, so I'd thought, and,
sure enough, the next day it was gone,
meal for an owl or a hawk, I assumed,
but as I came closer, my dull heart jittered
and paused, because on that bright spring lawn,
two small holes, newly dug, opened
another thought. Had it just been asleep

or taking in sun and filling its lungs
with fresh air when its mate scrambled up
and coaxed it awake with her chilly
mole-nose, and side by side they burrowed
back down to their dark, adventurous tunneling?

ON THE BODY: A ZUIHITSU

1. One afternoon at the gym I forgot my combination and they had to break the lock. I called home to Nancy to say I felt woozy—she'd better come pick me up.

2. The world forgotten, memory gone.

3. Driving home from La Fiamma's with a couple of pizzas, I stop at a red light and suddenly dozens of naked cyclists ride past. A peloton in the nude. Women and men, young and old, sleek, chubby, obese. Most with helmets on, some in underpants, but nothing more. One two-seater is ridden by a bare-assed father and son.

4. "The poet is always our contemporary." Virginia Woolf.

5. Over the take-out pizza, our daughter-in-law Carla said, "Yesterday I saw an injured bird on the road. It must have had a broken wing. And there was another bird, a crow, standing beside it. I couldn't tell if it was trying to help the injured one or just waiting for it to die so it could eat it. Two cars came by and swerved around it, but a third car drove right over it. And—this was what was amazing—when the wheel went over the bird it made a really loud sound—*really* loud—like shattered glass."

6. In the hospital, I said to Nancy, "So you came and picked me up at the gym and brought me here?" And she said, "Yes," but a few seconds later I'd forgotten her answer and said again, "So you came to the gym and picked me up and brought me here?" The same question over and over at least twenty-five times.

7. When I was two and a half, we took the train to Florida, and sitting across the aisle was a troop of sailors coming home from the war. One of them showed me card tricks that were way above my pay grade. Then he shuffled the cards and showed me how he did it. *That* I thought I might be able to learn. I figured we'd be together as buddies for the whole trip, but in the morning he was gone.

8. The past is a slow falling snowflake that lands on the pavement and melts.

9. When they decided it wasn't a stroke, they checked my heart with an echo-cardiogram. I lay on my side and watched it pumping on the monitor as Zach, the tech-guy, moved his transducer thingy around. I could see the blood flowing in and out. It showed as splashes of blue and red on the monitor.

10. The poem about the father goes back many years. Swayed by a wish for normalcy he moved us to the suburbs, an Ivy League of grass, a lake to visit and for teens to make out by, clean schools. Then he took the commuter train back to the city where he might have raised us. His life would have been easier, but he gave us the best as he understood it.

11. Zach is a big guy—former military, I guessed—and he was happy to talk about what he saw, always with the proviso that "This is just me," i.e. not a real cardiologist. But he thought my heart looked ok. The pressure was right and there was no sign of a prior heart attack.

12. As he was getting older, my father told me he was glad to find his sex-drive becoming less urgent. And the first time I called home and said I was staying over with a girlfriend, he calmed my mother down.

13. Our son's neurologist, Dr. O., has a strong Brooklyn accent. We told her what had happened to me and she quickly diagnosed it as *transient global amnesia*. "It only lasts a couple of hours," she said. "Repeating the same question over and over is the key."

14. Someone once called him "the salt of the earth," but later it turned out that he'd been abusing the women in our family for years.

15. Next day we read in the paper about a world-wide cycling event: "A celebration of the body in all its myriad forms."

PALLADIUM SEEDS FOR PROSTATE CANCER

He says their half-life, halved
and halved again, means that in half
a year they'll be used up. Meanwhile,
they'll boil and burn, taking the tumor down,
those jail-break cells, those riotous lost souls
with creepy witchy lethal minds of their own.

The cure is not as risky as the disease,
so leaving my loved-ones in the waiting room,
I lie between bolsters in a loose green gown,
half-conscious as he slits behind my scrotum,
inserts four dozen radiating seeds,
and sews me up again.

I dream of a distant airport, my arrival,
where, showing a luggage token to the guard,
I slip inside, but it's a maze, Palladian,
high-ceilinged, multi-stair-cased, and no telling
where the bags will be.

In the recovery room, a nurse
leans over me. How do I feel? she asks.
Any nausea? No. But my vision
isn't sharp. I doze till she returns.
"Can you wiggle your toes for me?"
and I say, "No." But when she lifts
the bottom of the sheet, ten feisty toes
like Black Forest gnomes alive to her suggestion
are mocking me and wiggling on their own.

MY PORTRAIT BY VAN GOGH

He scores deep lines in my face, the ditches
I abhor, then brightens the blue and speckles

the whites of my eyes. He twists my aging lips
in a sardonic grin. "Don't sit so still,"

he tells me, "it's a lie." Compliant, I take
out my pocket notebook, and begin

by noting how his hair in crimson knots
falls to the right and shows some scalp.

His apron's full of random strokes—the reds,
the greens, ochre, and indigo of spattered paint

and where he's wiped his brush—which now
he lays aside. His fingers lick dried blood.

A violent sensitive man who drinks a tun
a month and has the shakes. His visions of

the fires of hell absolve him for the flashy whores
he loves. My temperament is not like his.

My second thoughts are milder than my first
and then I think again. He laughs and spits

and tells me to sit still—"Jackass, hold your pose!"—
takes up a knife and scrapes away my nose.

LADY DIGBY ON HER DEATHBED, 1633

When does grief become wonder?

—Marianne Boruch

His dear wife died in the night,
so young, so lovely, but the color
gone from her cheeks
so they rubbed them to bring it back,
and called in his painter friend,

who posed her on an angle,
one eye slit open, as if
still sighted. Her lord never remarried.
The painting holds his grief.
Van Dyck lives on as well,

in shades of cream and white,
and the soft rose of her lips.
Since his object was to console,
he stepped back in time to
the moment before her death.

Being expert with folds and shadow,
he opened the purple drapes,
the darkness she lies between,
and laid gold trim on her blanket,
scattered petals on the sheet,

the damask blooms she loved,
whose sharp cinnamon odor
fills the spousal room and pricks
our nostrils too, as with barely a hint
of a smile she draws her final breath.

SELF-PORTRAIT WITH BERET AND ANGST

Who's that in the mirror? Let me clip his
drooping white moustache. His grizzled hair,
its few strands standing straight like grass
in the early light, needs a good mowing.

So in his late self-portrait, deeply creased
between the eyes, scored deeper with
the handle of a brush, Rembrandt's baffled stare.
His lips curl downward, worried and morose

as if the master's lost his nerve. Some say
financial blows which forced his move to
smaller quarters marred his self-esteem. Or was this
just an exercise in mood, a pose to set against

those haughty younger versions of himself—
"Old Man Demoralized"? It could be both.
About to come apart, still he painted with
candor and skill, then putting down his brush

and stepping back he sensed it needed one thing
more—the navy blue beret to hide his thinning
locks. Finished, did he grin with satisfaction
at the pudgy nose he'd captured once again?

THE VISIT

for Frank Soos (1950-2021)

Deep in a cliff-side cave, I pass an elk's hide
spread for sleep and enter a schoolroom
where I see you sitting in the corner,
dressed in sweat pants and a light blue shirt.

Your head is tilted to the side and there's
a cobweb fastened to one shoulder,
so you must have been sitting here a while.
You greet me, but your slow Virginia drawl

is hard to follow, fading like leaves on
a frozen lake when the first snow comes down.
We have unfinished business that will have
to wait because, as I know when I'm awake,

you're dead—struck down last month when your bike's
front wheel spun off and you fell and cracked
your skull. So in my dream I realize
with a jolt that I'm visiting your ghost.

I stare at my memory of who you were,
brilliant and kind, a writer and a teacher
to the bone, but the wheels of hope no longer
turn and your lessons are eclipsed by loss.

Still, you seem to wish me well, though your
long-limbed fatalistic shrug tells me I'll have to
get along without you, since like those friends
who've gone before you'll now be dead forever.

Waking, I see sun glancing off the river
where we once skied together, and as you
pull ahead of me again, dissolving
into air, my memories and woe are one.

THE BERNSTEIN PLOT

Green-Wood Cemetery, Brooklyn, NY

Up the hill where Washington's rough-cut men,
were out-flanked by the British, lost and fled
by dinghy in the night to fight again,
here where the city's blue bloods grave their dead,
we've trudged in the late August heat past wings
and needles, chiseled mausoleums,
marble cherubs (though no choir sings)
and found his marker, short on facts, which seems
hardly to grasp what deft band-master, splendid
on his more than life-size stage, the world, dreams
underneath; but at least the grass is tended,
bushes trim and ruddy rhododendrons—loud
but not too loud—bloom like a soulful Mahler standard,
flush among the fashionable crowd.

THE ABORTION: A ZUIHITSU

1. A friend needed an abortion that would cost $500. $500 was a lot of money in those days, but I had plenty in my bank account. I was supposed to be buying new clothes: shirts, ties, slacks, a winter coat, a sporty Ivy-league jacket. But I almost never bought new clothes. Clothes didn't interest me.

2. Thinking back through time, not just millions but billions of years and millions of generations, unspooling back through lemurs and fish to the earliest microbes, each individual contending, battling against the odds; then fast forward to us, brainy primates at the end of the line, and add up the odds against each of us ever coming into being and having a life.

3. My father would type his weekly letters to the *Times* on an old Royal Portable using two fingers. He could type faster with two than I can with ten. He kept carbon copies of all the letters in loose-leaf notebooks.

4. Abortions were illegal back then, plus she was Catholic. But it had to be done. She was just fifteen. My girlfriend set it up and went with her.

5. He rarely wrote about current events. Usually he had found a grammatical mistake, a poor word choice, or a factual error some copy editor should have caught.

6. The novelist Philip Roth liked to quote Czeslaw Milosz: "When a writer is born into a family, that family is finished."

7. The other night I dreamt that we had a tiger cub in the house. Orange-and black-striped, it played amicably with our two kittens. But where had it come from? The mother must be hiding out somewhere in the basement.

8. And the spawning continues. After we're done, our granddaughter will be happy to carry on.

9.   Once it seemed the function of poetry
      was to redeem our lives.
      But it was not. It was to become
      indistinguishable from them.

               —*Brenda Hillman*

10. We had double dated that past summer, which usually meant going to whoever's home was available and making use of the bedrooms.

11. In the dream I dropped by my friend Helen Frost's place, and asked what we should do about the tigers, but she shook her head and said she didn't know. Helen wrote one of my favorite sestinas called "Wandering Around, Getting Nowhere."

12. The boyfriend was also fifteen. So young to be a parent or even in that predicament. Why do I think of this now as my time is drawing toward a close? Am I seeking a verdict on my life?

13. Some problems aren't meant to be solved.

14. One of the *Times* editors lived in my aunt's apartment building and when she happened to mention my father's letters he perked up and said, "Not *the* Arthur Morgan?"

15. The operation was a complete botch, and afterward she bled and bled.

TO A SOLSTICE PARTY IN FAIRBANKS

A sun-swirl, egg-over-easy, with a swatch
of rainbow colors left and right
as the day-long winter evening fades,
Orion riding shotgun on the night.

But driving isn't easy on the ice,
and up a snow-packed hill the engine falters.
I back up blindly, landing in a snow-berm
with a jolt. Shaken, breathing deep,
I'm taken by an old refrain: how beauty
is allied with pain.
                    The moon's a flower
through a cage of spruce. Stars seed the night.
And soon a passing stranger stops
and frees me with a push—they usually do.

I shoot the hill again in second gear,
but when I rush the turn—default—
an unfamiliar driveway brings me to a cabin
where a sign warns:
                    "Killer Kats—Beware!"
I shout, "Hello?"…"Hello?"
The radio's tuned to folk but no one's home.

So backing slowly down the drive
I try the other fork…
                    bright lights,
a barking dog and voices, candles
flaming on a tree (our hostess guards
it with a pewter candle snuffer), as,
perplexed at how the north's adopted me,
I place my cooling moose stew on the board.

THE DRONE

At the pond off Goldstream Road
mallards, a golden eye, two tundra swans,
and a drone so loud it drowns out thought.

Four chopper blades at the corners,
the skipper in fatigues manning his remote—
what use are binoculars against such noise?

But we all have our games, our toys. Annoyed
at our annoyance, he packs it in, packs it
into his pick-up and drives off, leaving us

to bird in peace, as it comes back to me:
once as a kid, I filled a cardboard tube
with the heads of kitchen matches, covered it

in tinfoil, counted down. Smoke, flames
spouting from the nozzle, amazingly
it blasted off. House-high. Tree-high. Small

as a pencil stub against the sky. And came down
in a neighbor's yard, no damage done,
except when my mother missed her matches.

Don't you ever do that again! she said.
Today the universe grows wider than
we knew back then, as stars, our cosmic neighbors,

make their measured circuit of the night,
and I wonder if my days of rocket science
could have seeded me another life—

hidden in a bunker somewhere north of Vegas
targeting a village in the drone-filled Middle East,
a life of easy pickings, believing that

the dead don't feel the blast that killed them or
their kids. X marks their graves. A path
less radical than poetry, this sweet deceiver,
that perhaps someday I'll have to answer for.

THE METEOROLOGIST

Maybe you heard me say on the radio how I stepped out the front door and there it was,
less than a football field away and a mile wide, with barely time to rush inside and
slam the closet door when the house collapsed around me, roof joists, shards
of sheetrock imploding, then rising up with me feathered among shingles,
splinters, bricks—buffeted,
blinded, whirling in
sparks of blackness—
and I thought this
was it for sure, but
then it set me
down in a field,
—the neighbor-
hood gone and
several neighbors
dead—stunned
in the sizzling
silence after,
still alive though
battered by this
brutal bout of weather that I'd bantered about for years.

MT. RUSTY CARS

Tanana Lakes, Fairbanks, Alaska

The orange metal of abandoned axles, crumpled
hoods, radiators, fenders and parts unknown
like some cubist apocalypse after a war—

cars totaled on bourbon rollovers at three a.m.,
stockcars run off the track, pickups sliding
on icy pavements into a tree, or

the bloody upshot of a road-crossing moose,
all roped off and piled in a hillock, rust-orange
and brown on which a swallowtail

lazes taking in sun and where a sign
incised in birch declares with a wink,
"Mt. Rusty Cars," just as we hear

a fisherman shout, "Oh, shit!" for the big one
that slipped his hook. Our last time here
Ben spotted an eagle perched at the top

of a spruce. Now he's moved on into
his grown-up life, and like the couple we were
in our early years, we tread a path of our own—

this morning's walk meanders down
"Chickadee Lane"—taking our time and listening
to trills, a yellow-rumped warbler, and is that

a hermit thrush? Your cracked pelvis mended,
my prostate tumor tamed, yet they forewarn
like the riff you performed the other day

in a minor key, a requiem without divinity.
Last week a small plane went down in the hills
killing the pilot—the father of a friend—aged 81.

You say, "I don't even plan to be driving
a car by then." The whole of life comes
crashing to an end, but as the horizon angles in

precipitous, we cradle moments like these
as sunlight sparks through aspen and birch—
like holding a newborn granddaughter in your arms,
smelling her waxy scalp and kissing her sleepy eyes.

JUNIOR THE DOG

Retired, Sam Senior had worked with toothpicks
and glue to make a schooner that he slid into
a bottle, then pulled on a thread to launch its masts.
He'd also built a toothpick Ferris wheel with seats
that swiveled as it turned, but since they said
I couldn't play with it, I didn't see the point.

Their old house, heavy with rugs and over-stuffed
chairs had fancy candlesticks above
the fireplace and creaky stairs that curled
up to a powdery second floor. The smell
of Victoriana weighs on my mind because
Sam Senior was dead, whatever "dead" meant.

When I asked my widowed great aunt
where he was, she pointed toward the sky
and so I figured he'd become a cloud. My mother
said he'd had a heart attack which baffled me.
I knew the heart keeps pulses in your wrist
but how it could attack you was a riddle.

The mutt we found in their yard was
mostly spaniel. We brought him home with us
and called him "Junior the Dog" to honor
Sam Senior's scholar son who we called "Junior,"
but Junior the Man was not amused and said
that we should now just call him Sam.

Junior the Dog, a boring, friendly pooch,
was white with splotches of brown and droopy ears.
My cousin and I decided a firedog would be
more fun, so I held Junior by his tail (he hardly fought),
while Tommy got out our paints and painted him red,
which livened up our day when we got caught.

MANNY PERL AND THE SECRET WISH

Down the block, around the corner,
the longest walk I'd ever taken,
as he recited poems—Robert Service
and the one called "Gunga Din," *It was Din, Din, Din,*
With the bullets kickin' dust-spots on the green—
then, taking my tiny hand, my grandfather
led me across the lawn right up to it.

The well had a bucket, a handle to turn,
but we didn't turn it. Instead
he took a silver penny from
his pocket, one from the recent war,
and said I should make a wish and toss it in.

The stones mounted all the way to my chin,
so he hoisted me up so I could look
down to the water, but I couldn't think
of anything to wish for, since at that moment
the great adventure of my life seemed
just about complete. But he said again
that I should make a wish.
"But don't tell me what you wished for,"
Manny warned, "since that would spoil it."

A scientist friend insists
that there's no proof the past is real.
Our memories are full of errant turnings
and *Yesterday's gone*, as the songsters
have it, *Yesterday's gone*.
Only the present moment exists.

I couldn't hear the splash
but I saw ripples spreading. They spread
their ecstatic joy across the years
right up to today. Today
I can't remember what I wished for
and even if I did, I'm not allowed to say.

WITH MY SON AT TENNANT LAKE

for Ben

Under a forest of lilies bullfrogs croak
and muskrats steer between
roots like snub-nosed biplanes
skirting funnel clouds. That's why
they call this marsh a lake. Binoculars
in hand, we scan the far expanse of farms.
A mile-long coal train hoots by.
An osprey glides our way. Across its path
a red-winged black bird flutters nervously.

These active flyers bring my heart alive,
but then I flashback to last week
when you OD'd on seizure drugs
and launched into a manic rant: *My life
is on the line! Why don't you
answer me?* So to the hospital
where, unlike yourself, you flirted
with the nurses, but refused to pee
until a young one, flirting back,
said, *Please, for me,* and taking the green
bottle you sashayed into the john.

The brochure says the marsh, a former
swamp, is drying up, its future
woods. Like us. We've turned,
are turning with the passing years,
from sprouts to flowers to seed,
a tadpole then a frog, or in
my case from brown to gray.

The other night a frog clung to
the ceiling in my dream—
turquoise blue and green, some orange
too, wide eyed and staring down.

Its small toes' suction held it up
and when I got a broom and knocked
it off it fell into my hair. *Where is it now?*
I cried in panic, trying to comb it out.

Then waking I recalled the ones
we'd seen in Costa Rica years ago. *Don't*
touch!—sometimes beauty has
a toxic skin. That's what we face in life
and what great art can show. We rode
on horses to a swampy mud-bath place.
Then in the shower, you seized.
Your glasses fell and broke. We
patched them up with first-aid tape.

These days your seizures mostly controlled
by meds, you play in the local symphony,
get around by bus, and today enjoy the marsh's
spring-time orchestra—those frogs for bass,
the trills of birds above—*a tour*
de force we'd love to be a part of,
and in our brisk companionable way we are.

"AND NEVER LOOK BACK"

Two puny butterflies, elfins perhaps, flit
through the bushes, one in pursuit like a hot
summer romance…so unlike our two year
one-sided courtship, because you thought
I was 'taken' and we were just friends. So
the other evening when our granddaughter asked
how we met, you said, "In a group of high school
friends," but I broke in with my fiercer truth:
"It was love at first sight!" And the folks
around the table breathed out, "Ooh!"
Now those bugs are in another bush. One
hides while the other searches high and low.
The past unveils itself when fiery linkages
recur. He'll find her again, and off they'll go.

from

Spear-Fishing on
the Chatanika

THE DIVE-MASTER'S MANIFEST

Here is your wet-suit, your tank, this is
the weight-belt, your mouthpiece, your mask,
never called goggles. These are your fins,
not flippers, please, and this is the pressure gauge.

Lean back, let the tank pull you over,
and when you bob to the surface, point
to your head like this, making the sign for OK.
The rest is gesture. No sounds but the burble

of exhale, the sonorous inrush of breath.
You must never forget to breathe or the pressure
will shrivel your lungs to the size of a mango seed.
Quickly, as we descend through clouds

of insignificant species if your ears feel the weight
of water like heaven's thunder pressing in,
just hold your nose and blow,
as you would on a plane coming down.

A crab is a five-fingered crawl.
When I pinch with thumb and forefinger, making
this sign, observe the barracuda as it lolls
between ridges of coral like an overturned hull

covered with barnacles, covered with lime.
Brain coral's a frothy confection, its surface
of folds like gray matter on which the parrot
fish dine. Should my hands stand erect

as in prayer, beware the shark's silhouette
and mark how thought can shrink
at the sudden appearance of implacable design.
Note the delicate coral fans.

The swaying of fronds from the waves'
deflection at depths resembles a dance
that recalls how small ships in a gale
rock to the beat of the devil's quadrille

till your stomach heaves and throbs—
another adjustment you must make to
the deep, as at evening going to sleep,
your bed has the softness of coral, and shells

fill the blanks of your eye-holes,
the sighs of your breathing forgotten—
till a gasp, and you come to yourself
in the ever-remembering water.

SCOUTS SPEAR-FISHING ON THE CHATANIKA

Cross-legged on the bank around
a stylish blaze our fathers counted coup—
how beautiful from the air

those cities lit by bombs,
the giddy godless scare
of elemental flack, blue sequins

on the black. At dusk, we hit the beach
and slogged against the current in
our rubber wading breeches.

Cold, fast, slippery like the rush of
inspiration, whitefish burst
upon us, gleaming in our headlamps

like a spray of meteors. Laughing,
screaming, jabbing with our tridents, bloodying
the waters—not one caught.

They whipped right past and
vanished down the river like
guerillas with their terror into
existential darkness, or the silence of a thought.

A MAN WITHOUT LEGS

Foxes are common this year, kingfishers
perch by the river,
but today on the bikepath alone

a man without legs
hands briskly circling to power
his chair up the hill toward town

and I slow my car as I pass
his firm native face etched with wrinkles,
brown like the color of spruce bark,

his wide brimmed floppy hat
and ranger's camouflage
worn with a fluid grace

as the mine he must have triggered
a couple of decades ago
goes off again in my face.

ABOVE THE TANANA: FOR MURIEL MORGAN (1914-2001)

[Note: The Tanana River rises in western Canada and flows through central Alaska before joining the Yukon. A number of poems in this collection are set on a ledge overlooking the river, with a long view south to the Alaska Range.]

Against the river's westward flow, a brace
of mallards, as I scope them out, flutter
and swerve, full of their own quack-quacking

and a part of the dismal comedy
that spectral eagle all enmeshed in clouds
soars silently above. As the last of

last winter's snow melts from the mud-gray banks
an hour at this spot has given me back
my voice, and I recall, two months ago,

a continent away, as time wound down
to absence and beyond, your bed turned crib,
your eyes turned glass. For all that was witty,

lively, bright, sharp-honed—long nails pale blue, hands
chilled, words flown. With one eye shut, the other
lid half-down, that half of half a stare still

marked my place. Across the way a helicopter
prowls the flats, and up the river following
those ducks, a hooded boatman with his rusty mutt.

I glass them too then let them go. Your latest
gasp, to the cup of juice I held, was: "More,
more, more!" They say that hearing's the last sense

to fade. "But how would they know?" asked your
cynic friend, Helene. Still, I held your hand
and stroked it as you moaned. Below me,

a litter of branches and logs and scolding
from that spruce-top, one gray-backed harbinger
of spring. As tubing pumped the futile

oxygen, I partnered your agony,
whispered easing words to the unknown, and
squeezed a syringe of morphine on your tongue
that simplified your beauty to a stone.

MOURNING CLOAK

Fairbanks, June 9, 2001
for my son, Jeff, also a poet

Sandbars channeling the flow, a floatplane
skimming low above the river, and capping
the ghostly front range, purple avatars of snow.

Brooding on the strains of work and cash,
last night you called—one year of school to go—
and damned the tennis shoes that kids in

Guatemala make, whose lives we trample on.
I said, though better off, we still have labyrinths
of choice and chance to hunker through to shape

a life. A flicker on a tree trunk hammers
for a bug. Shaggy spruce logs dumped in shallows.
Smell of sage, no roses yet, an ancient

cola can blanched white, and moving in
behind a wobbly V of cranes, a late
Alaska jet. But why, you asked, do poets

speak a privileged tongue and paid-off schoolmen
skulk such shady paths? "Is everything political?"
I said, knowing the way a line turns on

itself has lots to teach of tact and tactics
in the greater world. But spurning the merely
personal, *"Bullshit!"* you explode. "So what

if my grandma's dead, and suppose I write
of it—who'll give a fuck?" I sucked in breath,
feeling my heart beat fast, orphaned again.

Last March at her rainy grave site among
the Orthodox, easing our hurt with Hardy's
darkling thrush, we shoveled on farewells of dirt.

And now, by luck or art, this butterfly
intrudes—a mourning cloak, near black with
golden fringe and sash of azure stars, a shred

of night by day. I hear the buzz of bugs
awakening to spring and watch a busy
moth, ants trailing up a branch. Like gravediggers

who forge their drastic living from the dead,
we schmoozed and argued half the night away.

A MEMORIAL PERHAPS

Hauled up by a crane, bright saxophone
girders erect themselves in sky, the steel
untwisting like an awakening god, and on
the unfolding floors carpets unroll, the odd
desk appears, and workers materialize
and rally around the coffee machines. A file
drawer opens releasing a puff of smoke.

Each cubit of air recalls the tremor
but not the flames, the shouting or
shortness of breath, and through this
transparency a man stands on a platform,
wiping his eyes and stretching into space.
There's nothing below him but morning
(no rattle of jets), as a flag goes up the pole.

Building down from the top, we've reached
the 93rd floor, where several aging veeps roll
up their sleeves and sip their 9 a.m. dram
of satisfaction, while how many knives in back
rooms sharpen for action and how
many cattle are driven to corporate slaughter?
(Nothing is bogus here, nothing made up.)

And everything's in plain view to the old
cleaning woman in the twin invisible tower
a bucket of suds at her side. The stench of
burnt fuel sponged off, and only the white and blue
of empty floors below her like some hopeful saw
(repent? forgive?) that might turn the world around,
which a wand like a thought can pass through.

When the supports gave way, the upper
floors came down intact. For fifteen seconds
weightless, they fell, like an elevator
with a snapped cable, on top of the pancaking
lower stories which crushed everything below,
but while this was happening, they were above
the disaster and rode it down to the ground.

THE BATTLE OF AUSTERLITZ

Wakened by a dissonant *drop*
drip, worked in the bathroom late,
adjusting the ball to give the rusty tank
its proper level, then
because the blanket was too thin,

pulled on a pair of socks
and read about African termites
in their mounds, and then
about the Battle of Austerlitz,
a novelist's account, turned out

the light and fell into a slumber.
At nine the doorbell rang,
he rushed downstairs. One of the
weekly students with her mom,
each with a violin,

but his teacher-wife was gone...
shopping, he guessed, annoyed.
Dialed her cell phone number.
She answered the second ring
and when he heard

her smiling at his voice
his fierce heart melted,
but she murmured, "Dear,
you need to come and get me,"
her weak voice sinking at

the end. And dizzy with sense of
creeping age, of something
gone spectacularly wrong, groans
of the dying, woke up
to this rainy winter's day.

POET CHARGED IN SCRAPE

*"The Coast Guard charged Poet
with negligence in the accident."* A.P. (3/11/98)

As the ferry approached Morse rock
    it was growing dark and the navigator
sighted on a tree he'd marked on his chart

a year or so before. The moon was low
    and each ripple had tiny sickles
darting at its peak and his name

was Daniel Poet and he thought
    his life had turned into a dream,
sailing this ferry through a narrow

breach where mountains and glaciers
    shifted on their pins like drunken tars
and whales were floating islands lolling

on the waves. His thoughtlessness
    did not cost lives and only a little meaning
spilled through the crack in the hull

that Poet made. Darkness and other trees
    obscured his reference point
when the ferryboat Aurora scraped Morse rock,

the Coast Guard said.

JETSAM

Blue of the water, blue

of the sky, a lighthouse
steeped in sun. Wearing my
sweater backwards I pass

between narrow structures
of air to the beach. Starfish,
bottles, shoes, a sharkskin
glove without a hand.

From kindergarten on
in constant love with one
small girl or another—
barnacles, china shards
of a death—girls full of

driftwood and the
passionate scent of the shore
(no rhythm holds these waves)—

because of this, I believe
in nothing, can violate no laws.

Stretched on the sand I drowse,
clutching a shell as if
only its echo tied the ocean
down, when suddenly a spark

smudging itself to a seawall,
swirling in air calls me home:

my eyes a web of light,
pinned on my back I wake,
a lost fact on the beach,
wreck of the 'I'

that loved those luminous girls.

WHISTLER'S MOTHER

One foot on a rail of
the porch, he drinks
sparks from a glazed brown
mug. His day was luckless, a
black and white occasion.

Uncomfortably red, he
watches the sun setting
along the breast of the hills
like a part of himself
broken loose, the difficult

capture of evening in a net.
"Don't go fishing at
night," his mother would have
said, cautioning against all
the chances he'd had to take.

Of course she wished him well.
Heroic in the suburbs,
he'd spoken his piece,
strolled out the door
and encountered a fate.

In the long run there was
this: an island, a boat,
and time's dark belly of
stars. Cheerful, flirtatious,
the night-birds sewed their

shadows to her tender
silhouette, while the hours
piled up like sketches
in a bottom drawer, perfected
and abandoned like the leaves.

TIME OFF FROM BAD BEHAVIOR

An outlaw can't be outdoors
all winter long. He needs to
go home to his wife,

sit around, drink cocoa
on the couch. It is night
somewhere deep in the last

century. There are more
stars over Kansas than marshals
at Fort Knox. Time

to plot the next
great raid. Time to relax
in the pure pleasures

of the criminal mind.
Those shadows slinking down by
the edge of the field: cows

from the Capital of Missteps,
or some would-be brave neighbors
scouting a reward. No one

comes within range. Who
has the gumption to face
a man with a smile so quick

all you'll see is the bottom
of the sky falling into your lap
as his jaunty dog lopes by.

ANGLES RATHER THAN ANGELS

What was odd inside the dome were all
the angles, lacking roundness, in the stifling
air, as we slogged up single-file past
easy breathing, each corner crammed
with fagged-out pilgrims fanning, and
glanced through ordinary panes of glass
at tiled roofs with concrete buttresses,
which showed the engineering, not the blessing,
after all that holy glitter down below,
and finally emerging at the bell,
gazed upon a miniature city
which seemed a blowsy fresco of itself,
yet almost natural, under an egg-shell sky,
as if it simply grew there like a rose.

REVOLUTIONARY POETS

1.
An engineer, a waiter, a man
who lived with his mother.
Either he smoked cigars, or
someone made that up.

2.
Once her steamfitter father
saw a pipe explode and
bake a room of men. He said,
though they didn't know it
they were dead. Their legs
carried them out the door
and into a parking lot
before the over-done meat
began to peel from their bones.

3.
See his blueprint for a universe
which contracts as it cools.
There, the moon is a mirror
made of dust, a doll
shaken till one eye sticks open.

4.
We cringe at their beauty,
their intolerable strength.
They curl around our dreaming
heads, another spiral galaxy
of char. One says,
"The feet are as blind as the ears
but less rigid." Another declares,
"When you have followed my compass
to this shovel, bury
your shoes and float away."

THE DENALI WOLF

Near the East Fork of the Toklat
in the season that's never dark
I lugged my gear back from the road

and while I slept through dusk
a noise like trash in the suburbs
being clattered away woke me up.

When I stuck my head out of the tent flap
the hoofed creatures were gone
but what I saw at eye-level,

like a fury sculpted in ice
brought me to my knees.
Once I'd wanted to paint a canvas

some huge fanatical blue
where the hungers of the world
could settle and be soothed.

Ten feet away, ears pricked
nose flaring, the silver-gray
pursuer stared me in the face,

then sensing I wasn't prey
whirled off along the river,
and I watched him shrink to a point

in imaginary time
fleet as the fastest athlete
I'd ever seen in my life.

NEPTUNE'S DAUGHTER

Two sons come home on a bus, but
she's unaccounted for, left
behind on shore. I chide
the lady driver who should
have counted. And then—
cartoons of fish debating
on TV; people are arriving
for a party. Still no daughter.

Paint cans, plants in pots,
a rake. I try to extract
our green car from the
cellar. At last it stands
in the driveway of my youth
but where will I go to
find her, what if she
isn't there, my dashing daughter?

Later she returns, gracing the
prow of a yacht. Five
years old, her face gray
as snow, a bitter fact no
one could love enough. What
have we done to
distort her emotions, oh my
daughter, my daughter!

With mouth closed over water,
she has a trick to play.
The night is getting old; brutal
dawn will carry her off,
but the dampness lingers.
In my dark red blanket, I
huddle like the riddle of a
god who lost his daughter.

AT THE FARMHOUSE IN WEST BRANCH (1965)

for Bob Grenier

Your guests had to wade through
a pig-sty, so you'd greet us at the gate
and prod those massive porkers out of the way
with the handle of a broom.

In back of the rented house, we strolled
in the shade of walnuts and mused on
our trade, while you bagged the fallen fruit—
which wasn't like stealing, you said,

since they'd only rot on the ground.
Inside, you laid out the treasures
you'd picked up last summer at Groliers,
the latest Ashbery teasers and another

little-known poet whose bare-boned
fluted quatrains, cold
as the Minnesota sky, you'd squint
and cackle at. You read the world

like that—through the eyes
of poetry—until sky and piglets and
walnuts (which Emily baked into pies)
unshackled my bookish soul

and my love began to unfurl
the first acceptable stanzas
I ever wrote, while Emily,
as her pregnancy advanced,

jotted on greasy napkins,
God knows how, the knock-out
poem of the year in the bitchy
fastidious voice of a mother sow.

MEN TOO

Under your left nipple, something hard.
The doctor gawks. It happens to men too,
unhealthy flesh congeals and
spews its microscopic seeds into the lymph.
The face in the mirror blackens and disappears.
A world without self, swings
like a hanged man from an endless noose.

The mammogram you have in one of those loose
paper gowns is inconclusive, the surgeon
dubious. But better to cut than dangle.
A blue sheet tenting over your head conceals
the blade's caress, the rush of blood. The nurse
sponges it up. Your mother wanted a
daughter first. Welcome to the sisterhood.

ABOVE THE TANANA: FOR JIM SIMMERMAN (1952-2006)

"Landscape is an after-thought, like hope."—J.S.

Sun ratchets off a fish-wheel like machine-
gun spray. An airboat blasts upriver

flaunting the rack of a dismantled moose.
An island like a coffin floats off-shore,

and black spruce grow from it, green rockets
questing skyward like the piquant vows I've made

while sitting on this shelf—to trust in life,
not death. Two months ago you put an end

to pain though I just heard today. Grief takes
my skull, noon spins toward dusk, dim lights on

water, murky shapes, dissolving branches,
slime the river carries as your corpse decays.

Oh, Jim! I've sifted the peevish facts—two
hip replacements failed, your last pooch given

away, a recent love estranged—you'd been
to hell and back—and so on whiskey and

what else you pulled the curtain, left us
here to plumb the tale. This was the summer

of yellow-jackets, of wasps and fatal stings.
A whale got beached and rotted sixty

miles from here, six hundred from the coast.
These aberrations clustered round your death.

And paging through your letters (back when
we wrote such things) I found a sly request

for "one of those river poems." No urgency
I'd figured, figured we'd grow old together

in the craft, mellow like two peppers in
a pot, or like some aging boy band, you

on bass and me on uke. Four days you lay
alone, four days. I hold my breath and

see that jaunty walk and cheeky grin
shut down. You'd seemed a buoyant optimist,

an army brat, black belt and softball buff,
but under those riffs a darker music

thrummed. I heard it louder the last time
we met, as, antsy, less in focus on

your meds, you pulsed a hunger to be
somewhere else, to step outside your pain.

The pain I couldn't see. I see it now,
that slough in which the self begins to drown.

PRESERVE YOUR FAMILY PHOTO ALBUM ON-LINE

This naked infant prone on the dressing table
is who? And "Evelyn" in
the couple aligned with your folks?

In mortal disorder, this slideshow of
kinship washes across the screen—
a father in uniform, the son by

his side leaning shyly into his hip,
and how to deal with these
brilliant swan-like lovers caught in a swoon

their lips in the ambient light an inch
apart, who in a flash will be gathered with
generations on the convertible couch

as a creepy decrepitude sloshes
across their faces and fir trees whip
and bow in the seascape above

their heads—like this cruel offending thought:
our time too will be ending.
The Perl nose, the Morgenstern

chin—Tony like Peter, Manny
like Tom, and three babies together
under the shade of a bush, riding their scribbled

nicknames like toy boats. Only that rabbi
out of a Polish past, proud in his
Sabbath regalia, his carved medieval chair,

stands for a burnished order, aloof from
this flux of familial parts
with his beard rippling down his chest.

WAZZAT?

The trouble with subject, he said,
—it crimps the results and pins them
rigid like diamonds, but not
                        the pretty ones—
hard industrial tools, like those things they wrapped
leather around to make shoes before
there was plastic...
                        —when suddenly like a shushed
whisper or gasp, a
scrabbling above us in the gutter, and then

not a bird. A bat?—no. Not anything, yet
something, what?—launched like a fur hat on the air,
and then like a pale blue rat racing up, up, up,
and sailing off again into the dusky night, smack

into another tree, lands on the trunk, and dashes
again, up to the launch point and spreads its
what? Not wings, sails?—its cloak, or

webbing, this wild webbed dandy from a planet
once called Earth we'd heard remote and faulty rumors of.
Again it lands, takes off, glides, lands in a spruce and disappears
among the hazy branches of our disbelief.

KINDLING: For Ben

[Note: In epilepsy, *kindling* refers to the process by which seizures
propagate through the brain and induce future seizures.]

In this thicket of nerves, unstable tinder,
a synapse near the hippocampus sparks
the neuron tree to flames, and your hands'

slight tremor sharpens to a jiggle, then
a shake, eyes darting right, chin pitching
upward in a baffled double-take

as wildfire spreads. You groan, then gurgle,
gag, a whirlpool burbling in your throat,
your grin satanic, not you but like some thug

who'd cut throats in back alleys, lead a
holocaust of souls to hell—O hell!
what do mine eyes with grief behold, lost

in the brutal shark's mouth of your spell!—
Grasping beneath your arms, we lower
your jittering weight, settle your legs

out straight, as shakes become a
           general quaking,
check
    our watches—seconds passing into

evil grace, the self
           absconded, lost
a

total abandonment this
           jerking, thrusting,

                then a sudden
                        which could be

endless, then

        you toss your head, blink, mumble, gaze
        into the moment, nod "Um-hmm" to
        half-a-dozen questions, not finding

        words but wending back through
        fire-charred acreage, ash and smoke,
        from another irrevocable attack.

AN EASY DAYHIKE, MT. RAINIER

for Nancy, Jeff and Ben

Bright mushroom clouds of yellow lilies flame
at Eunice Lake where under jutting peaks,
we snack and muse on Jeff, our older son,

who studies poetry, the climbing art that twines
the word with time, then note fresh deer tracks in
the mud as switchbacks steepen into blueberries.

The lookout tower's locked but we can see
through glass, a gas stove, bunks, a log book
(1986-93),

as drizzle comes. We linger, hoping
that the mountains will de-cloud and talk about
Ben's seizures, never tamed—a recent one

that spun him down the hall, whirled him into
a concrete wall. The school nurse found him
on the floor, knocked cold. I got the call and

in her office—blood dribbled from his nose,
beside his eye a crimson bruise, one tooth
a vicious fang, one broken straight across,

he sat and hardly moved. The razor ridge
to Tolmie Peak, we skip, and so descend
through old-growth deliquescing under rain.

At Eunice Lake again, the deer himself
stares back across his shoulder at our stares.
Later, Ben's dentist sealed the pulp, squeezed

plastic from a tube to patch the cracked
stalactites in his mouth. Headache gone,
he took it patiently, while black light

hardened plastic into tooth, or almost tooth.
As we approach the trailhead, sun breaks through.
A rainbow lies on Mowich Lake. It floats

beneath our feet—a sign perhaps, though who
believes in signs? The world is flux, each day
a setting forth. Our trip's a cache of weathers

like the sky. Six hours into this 'easy
hike,' wasted and refreshed, we reach the rented
Sunray, drink our Diet Cokes and split a peach.

Archives of the Air

I

ARCHIVES OF THE AIR

This guy who knows more about cranes
than they know about themselves
   (because their brains
are thumbnail small) explains that the sandhill's

call—a loud rattle and a squeak—comes not from
one crane's beak but two, the male's note answered
   by his mate's.
Also, he states, when one of them croaks,

the survivor often hangs around for months
and mopes, and here he relates the story of
   a grieving
female in the DMZ between the

two Koreas, rescued at great risk
by South Korean troops and shipped to him in
   Maryland, though
the law forbids it, yet she arrived

safely and briefly joined his local set.
He's the one who, using ultra-lightweight
   planes with crane
insignias, teaches home-bred whooping

cranes to migrate. Whoopers are less endangered
thanks to him. He raised one female from
   the egg and,
wearing a crane costume and pointing his beak

to the sky while flapping his fake crane wings
and jumping up and down, coached her in
   the mating dance,
but when someone jokes, "Sounds like a fine

romance," our self-styled *crane-iac* shakes his head.
"Totally boring," since he had to be
          outfitted and at
her beck and call whenever she wanted to ball.

Nestlings keep their distinctive peep for
a year, though fully grown by then,
          so the family unit
holds through one full cycle of migration.

They ride the mile-high winds with a sixth
magnetic sense that returns them to the acre
          where they began,
a skill that puzzles even our crane man.

As we circle the field, watching through our scopes
the long-legged, red-capped semi-prehistoric crew,
          scuffles and
skirmishes erupt and feathers ruffle,

some lower their shoulders and crane their necks
suggesting flight. Some glide in low and land
          while others take off.
"If the chill is strong," he says, "perhaps tonight."

NOVEMBER SURPRISE

Fairbanks, Alaska

Ten below and ice-mist on the river
when "Oh," she says, "a butterfly!" as it
comes wobbling from the sun-room, settles
on the floor. We offer sugar water
in a spoon and watch its sucking tube unroll.
It sips, then flutters to the windowsill
and folds its scalloped wings against the chill.

By noon, bright sun, and full of spunk it beats
against the glass, in love with light. The ground
outside, a spanking white, looks welcoming.
Its wings, like paisley, red and brown, quiver
as it paws the pane, embodiment of
summer in late fall, cold-blooded thing,
whose hopes will never be this young again.

FROM A JOURNAL

[Note: this poem and the two that follow are based on the journal
I kept while serving as writer-in-residence at Denali National Park]

Woke to heavy rain, low clouds,
the wet-rag sky wrung out
with little hope for change. But hey—

it's the park. Let's go.
And driving toward Eielson, the rain
does change—to snow.

There on a hillside, a mother
grizzly playing with her cub—
delighted with each other

and by the frosty white,
they roll and wrestle in it.
At Eielson, a snowball fight

pits kids against the giddy bus
dispatcher. We take a hike.
And later hike again near

Stony Creek, noting a mound
of grizzly scat beside
a stretch of torn up ground

where the ravenous bear
rummaged turf for
ground squirrels—earth

gouged, mined, ripped, rocks
tossed aside like
ping-pong balls, a thorough

thrashing of the region.
Wild nature on a tear
alters our perspective (after

the playful grappling of
mother and cub) on the crushing
strength and menace of a bear.

VISION

Followed a fox toward Polychrome Pass.
Red smudged
with black along its lean rib-cage,

it rubs its muzzle on a former meal,
ignores the
impatient poet on its tail.

Then nearing the overlook, sun shearing
through low clouds
transmutes the view to glitter. Everything's

golden, scintillant. I feel like a seedpod wafted
into space and
check my shaky hands on the steering wheel.

As the road crests over its top, boundaries
dissolve. Beside that
sheer intractable edge, I greet my radiant center,

discharge all my terms. How easy it seems
to channel between
worlds, my old self dying into a new,

with nothing firm to hold me here
but love. And that's
what nature has it in its power to do.

THE HEAD

Nature, great creator, full
of invention, fabrication.

Day ten, went for a good-by look
to the bank of the East Fork, glacial

river, thick gray water. Suddenly
a head pokes up. A fish, an

otter? There's no telling—
barely seen, it vanishes.

Dream? Illusion? Was it
just a mental bubble?

But then that same queer
head pops up again, followed

by the long-necked mottled
body of a duck. Duck in a panic,

flapping, paddling, launches
a mad-dash for shore, and seems

about to make it when
the silted channel swallows it again.

ABOVE THE TANANA: FOR MALI GERGELY (1885-1966)

[Note: The Tanana River rises in western Canada and flows through central Alaska before joining the Yukon. Several poems in this collection are set on a ledge overlooking the river, with a long view south to the Alaska Range.]

The fire that over-wintered under snow
spills smoke in front of the front range, stunts
the view, a ghostly scrim on which I picture you,

a rush of life drawn from your years of struggle
toward belief. A swallowtail flutters past,
and catkins float from cottonwoods like

wintry rabbit's feet. Searching the web the
other day I found your bio, mistranslated
by machine. It called you "he" and fumbled

every verb. Still, I learned you studied art
in Paris, probed the folk-ways of
your native Hungary and when the

democratic revolution crashed you wrote:
"Each soul must find its path alone, since
all collective deeds dead-end in flames."

Pasque flowers gone, no roses yet. The slough
has taken half of its guarding island out and
the restless flow's eroding south. Exiled to

Austria, you fled again from Hitler's gang
and wound up in New York beside the El.
Up two flights, a reek of turpentine and oils

(at nine, I shrink back, pinch my nose),
you perched among us in a flowered smock,
painting and smoking Camels without stop,

the ashes drooping, falling to your lap.
You lined the colors up and prepped
our canvases, then let us go our way,

but when I needed help—a mallard's wing,
the tint of blue for sky—you sensed my wish
to paint elation not just bird, and conjured up

a lilting pool of sky. Then after class,
unknown to us, you plumbed another art.
A raven's shadow drifting past, a kestrel's

sharp alarm. This braided glacial river's not
a place you'd ever want to take a dunking in.
I googled up the grave in Budapest

that holds your ashes and pays tribute to
your works: the textiles, poems, paintings,
and the celebrated novel of your later years.

Ash—the smoking got you in the end. You said,
"I wouldn't want to be among the blessed
unless the animals can be there too."

ALIEN CORN

My aunt Ruth's shucking corn with us. It's odd.
She takes a knife and shears the kernels off, to
fry them like her mother used to do,
but I say, "No. We're cooking *on-the-cob*,"

and wake up knowing that my aunt's long dead.
Then lines recur from Keats' great ode where corn
and Ruth are linked, when "sick for home she stood
in tears…" I had it once by heart… "Forlorn!

the very word is like a bell," and ruth
and grief are synonyms of sorts. The night
is dense with them—loved relatives and friends
who, gone by day, are agents of a twilight
state, deep spies who tout a counter truth
and shadow us until the grieving ends.

THE GOOD LIFE (A DREAM)

Relaxing on lawn chairs beside the Jordan
River, we take in a lecture on how
in the olden days some clever Roman found
papyrus strips encrusted with sand
and baked hard by the sun, and thus brought forth
Sheetrock. And I ask my friend Dave if he's
ever wondered how many discoveries
and nifty inventions of great worth

must have accrued over the eons
for us to lounge in comfort here today.
Amazing, he agrees. Then, drawing near to
the river, I thrust my foot in, thinking, *Lo—*
this is it, that most blessèd of streams,
as my soul flares up and I am blown away.

UNDER YUCATAN

A gap in the jungle floor without
a marker, but pushing the bushes
aside—"This cave is about to be
famous," says our guide, leading us down
a rusted ladder to a pool we
wade through in our wet-suits, then around
a corner: spikes and needles of rock
and a massive limestone column blinking
with bats, mid-lake. "The rock is fragile,
please don't touch," he tells us, as we stroke
and splash beyond the column, dipping
under open-eyed where blind fish dart
within a blue so fiendishly trans-
parent we can see their beating hearts.
We drift and paddle, awed, lose touch with
the bottom, dive and swim among the fish,
whose souls we can almost see, if fish
had souls. "Look up." Our guide directs his
flare at the roof's repeating zigzag
hex, a figure seared by lamp-oil near
a sheltered ledge stained red. What rites, what
blood-lettings happened here? He shakes his head.
"Now make a circle please, turn off your lamps."

*

My mother dead, and
friends and cousins gone.
Those hapless towers
trashed, long wars begun,
unending twisted
times, always the future

like a scroll of necessary
chances that we stumble
into, blind as fish
in caves we can't
swim out of, caged in
labyrinths of loss.

*

He turns his lamp on and we fill our lungs,
blink, sucked back into light's bright gift of
presence, greet each other, parents, children,
friends, these cherished apparitions, caught
in time's intractable embrace.

MT. TAMALPAIS

for Nancy

*"When an excursion is proposed, all sorts of dangers
are conjured up, filling the wilderness with Indians, bears,
snakes, bugs, impassable rivers, and jungles of brush, to
which is always added quick and sure starvation."*

—John Muir *(Picturesque California, 1888)*

Beyond the firehouse, past the water
tower, the old trail thins and darkens.
Starbursts and lupines, bluebells, as we
climb (Aline your cousin, you, me, Ben
nineteen) toward the rustic string of cabins
Ali summered at when she was small.
We meet a guy who's hiking to the coast.
And what will he do there? Ali inquires.
Just camp and watch for whales. Last year by
the ocean, I recall, we saw a big-
eyed octopus blanch white and move in
on a white anemone, caressing
with suckered tentacles the lovely
plant-like beast, which shrank back on its rock,
drew in its fronds, and sat there like a
squishy volleyball. Cross-species love
is not assured of course. Reaching the homely
lodge we greet the resident tabby, break
out picnic lunch and you recount how Ben,
last spring, racked by another seizure,
fell and one plastic tooth came loose, then
heading for the dentist got confused,
phoned home and we pulled out our map.
He read us street names, we said take a left.
(In the age of the cell phone you can't
get totally lost.) Ben has a Coke,
I buy a hot chai tea, while you and
Aline share some bottled fizz, and we

head down. Suddenly weaving across
our path, these copulating dragonflies—
he rides on her back, tail curled under
like a teacup handle. They sally by,
a sampan gliding on a lake, come
gracefully about and pass again,
a breath away. But later that afternoon
at Max's retro 50s-style cafe
with Fats & Elvis on the mini-juke,
Ben complains his faulty memory
screws him up at school. Back in fifth grade,
each flag and capital, and all the books
he'd read were easy to recall but now
scarred neurons block key sectors of his
brain, new facts evaporate and solids
turn to mush. He squints into this absence
of yesterdays, an attic of empty shelves,
the tyranny of now. It drives you
frantic with a parent's tangled love,
but shaky on the past he plays his
violin with skill and looks ahead
with humor and ripe moods that make him
still himself. Remember
L.A. on that winter break, we'd seen
La Brea and the Rodin show, and
on our sixteenth anniversary
you took the tiger seed into your womb,
a deed of blood and of desire. Something
from nothing when the semen took. Whatever
turned up, we would live with that. The mind
strays through these primal woods, impossible
to say I am this thing that was, trails
winding among shadow with no final
destination we can name. Big ones
come down and block the path and rot and feed
the soil. O fabulous legends, captious distances!
We wander here together in the dusk.

THE ATTACK

As I ambled down-yard
toward the strawberry patch
where berries bunched

like tiny pink seed-pearls,
it snatched at my hair, raking
the skin beneath with

needle claws, thinking it
had bagged a perfect source for
nest-making or even a whole

ready-made nest wafting
past bluebells and wild roses
through its yard, and when

my brazen hand grazed by,
shouting a raucous *"Dee-dee-
dee-DEE!"* in my ear as if

I had no right to my own hair,
reluctantly the insolent
black-capped thug let loose
and flitted back into the spruce.

THE UNSAFE HOUSE

Waking after the dream to a slick
December gloom (a threat of end-time
hovers around the room), he goes
over the escape route, knowing the
attackers, a posse of children
with rifles and machetes, could smash
down the closet door, and find his
family huddled there, then finish them off
with a few brisk rounds to the head.
Better instead to scramble up through
the ceiling access way and into
the space below the canted roof
where they might go undetected,
and as he sits up and starts to dress—
a sickle moon slash-sinister in
the west—it comes to him that they
can make it up there using the bureau
drawers
        for steps
             and closing
                  them behind,
so that once they've replaced the sheetrock
ceiling door they could wait it out in that
unlit frigid space. But they'll need extra
sweaters—*hurry, for God's-sake hurry!*—
as the enemy rabble is breaking
into the house like they do, it seems,
on a daily basis in those far-off
desperate places where justice and
mercy have lost their cachet and life
holds much less value than in our dreams.

HOMELESS IN SEATTLE

Slouched in front of Bartell Drugs,
resting her chin on a man-sized crutch,
hat pulled down, she dozes where

yesterday standing tall, she laughed
and razzed the passersby, living on
that tattered edge you walk past fast

fists in pockets, cross the road
to where he sits legs stretching out
in sandaled feet and skews your path

under the painted yellow arch
asking for "the price of a Mac
in change" who yesterday you saw

slip behind that bush to pee. And this
unnerving youth with hair as long
as yours, a glint of jagged teeth,

who comes at you arms wide, hands
crooked and fingers pointing down—
"Get down!" he yells (you circle round),

"What the fuck you doin'? *Fuck!*"
Living solo at the invalids' hotel,
hot flashes, no libido, diarrhea,

sleeping not so well (rude facts
that overrun your fate), each
day for the allotted spell you lie

beneath a plastic artifice of sky
whose faded summer lake-side blue
you gaze at drifting in and out of time

while the clattering machine
slings its life-affirming rays that
take your raging prostate tumors down.

CELESTIAL FIRESTORM

Its green arc flares, swings low, crinkles, snaps
while stars behind glint through like sequins on
a shawl. *Where does it come from?* he asks.

                                 The sun,
you say, *I think*, pull onto the shoulder and step
out into chill. *But we only see it at*
night. Does it happen in day-time too and we
just can't see? It riffles, billows, flaps
like a pennant although there is no breeze.

His eyes dilated, dazzled by this binge
of fractiousness beyond our steady state,
plumb a strange new paradigm of space.
Drawing back, it slings a swarm of arrows tinged
with pink. You duck. It points a warning finger:
Look out, mortals, things could get much worse.

POSTCARD FROM NANCY

As companion to the Crivelli, a Vermeer
with your sad hand full
of worries on the reverse. This
too from the Gardner:

a young Dutch lady performs at the virginal.
A gallant gentleman, his
back to us, lends one ear
to the music, while

his other attends a blue dressed matron's
account. Inevitably
the checkerboard floor; and
in the left foreground

a bass viol had been laid down next
to a draped desk.
Is he a soldier?
Beside the quill

and parchment, could it be that those
are coins? Why
in such a domestic
scene does Caravaggio's

prostitute laugh on the wall above the music?
This painting filled
with lightly arrested motions
may offer us repose,

in hope that, not in despite of the world,
our music, when I
escort your viola, will hold
us counterpoised.

My diamond for his guilders? No. No brokers, Nancy.
In this age of
war and purchased love
mine's a free answer.

Iowa City, 1965

II

ANALECTS *(a gathering of literary fragments)*

ANALECTS OF THE RED CANOE

"Greedy for happiness, which he saw as an endless
succession of sunny afternoons..."—Proust

Sparks slide on the water, leap up
like fire stirred with a stick, as we heft
   the canoe over boulders into the bobbing
current.
         A neon flash of insect wings,
and around us downtown Fairbanks, Sunday,

     pushing noon—a log church steeple sheathed
in metal, and the gaudy purple Chena View Hotel.
Sweatshirts stowed under seats, Nancy
   steers at the stern:
                "Warn me if you
see rocks." At the bow my knuckles scrape

the side. Beneath—dissolving branches,
   rocks, the slime on which the river glides
eliding fact and
               looking, as our four orange
   life jackets sluice beneath a bridge
where lovers sketched bold deeds on gray concrete.

Ben waves to a passing green inflated raft
   and resting lady double-kayakers. Gnats,
mosquitoes,
         dragonflies. Grass and
willows sparse on the muddy banks,
   as I trail my fingers in a melt of

glacial implications sliding toward
some vaster chill. Iced to the wrist,
I wipe them on my pants.
                          A swallow spins
on sharp wingtips shaping effortless
    foliations in fast flight, and soon

the power plant, a steel-blue grizzly
    rampant on our left. Coal cars to
the right, while just
                        above us coal chunks,
scuttling, ride a screened-in belt across.
"Look, Ben," I point, recalled by the stench

    of ash to Rockaway: black barges docked
beside Jamaica Bay where another power plant
rising from
                    infancy vents its paternal
rage. The inward mind's not thought itself
    but shapes the senses resonate in matter—

tangible spirit—nerve taking on a new
    design, as wandering its grid of town,
the river carves an eighth dimension.
Lit from below the
                        bridges shimmy; backyards
    sprout their primary swing-set patios

the avenues concealed, and the legal
    artifice of lots breaks down. Whose tabby
lounges on whose cord of wood, stacked
    between car-ports? The buzz
                            of a float-plane
fades, and the roar of something raw around

the bend ripples the river's chronic afternoon.
Two speedboats dash up-current. Jeffrey
    calls out, adding his
                    weight to the roll,
as Nancy yells, "Sit still!" seeking our balance
    in their chilly wake. And, churning, I remember

    Guy Lombardo racing on Jamaica Bay when
I was three. I saw him
                flip his boat
and spit out flame, I saw his nearly mortal shape
lifted to sirens up and
              carried limp away.

 Sun flashes a sandbox, a plastic loader, pots,
    and trucks: you know the castle in your games
has such a moat—
            sluggish, cold, and filled
with glamorous teeth. Why mope—this world is
    so damn full of menace: even a rabbit, Ben,

or a canoe. Like an infestation of stigmata,
    gnats, blue and luminous, drift above a glare
of discordant sensations:
               brown icy water
under the brightest sun glazing our skins. Jeffrey
takes a paddle and joins in. Ben
             rows with a stick.

Ducks in a small cove nervously watch us go.
    No houses now on the banks, just grassy fields
with fireweed and vetch.
            Even before its
    roar, a massive Japan jet in front of us
takes off—grows small. And in its softening wake,

the hum of water on the hull, a swish of paddles,
    voice of a child who tells himself about
the shells of robins and of snails.
                         Occasional
traffic rumbles, shouts, the rhythmic tapping
    of a distant tape-deck. Amid the random music

    of what is, the family in canoe turns restless,
then relaxes, paddles,
                 rests, and finds it has no
destination it can name. Just here, just
                     now, under one
    specific, sheep-shaped cloud, the pastoral afternoon
becomes itself. We drift into our contrapuntal lives.

And drowsing I perceive him—scraggly bearded,
    dressed in torn old corduroys and patched
plaid shirt:
            a counter-self who missed the channel,
    got mired in some dead-end slough. He fled the draft
to Canada and then to Fairbanks—comes to himself

at forty-four, a hunter, trapper, not at home
    with other men. Alone in his barn, everything
logged to one side: books
               on a legless couch
beside a jug, a hotplate, the half-unfinished kennel
    akimbo on its pick-up. So easy
                   to come apart—

    just liquor and pills and floating pains that
stun him in the night. He
               lies on his back
    and watches the ceiling crawl. How fragile
the skin of today? And no one
               brave enough to face
what nature's maker really thinks of us,

invaders of the air. Our traffics of corruption
    ooze along the curb. Out in the yard, trees
charred where fire gripped
                        their bark surround
a flowery emptiness. Ragweed climbs its stem.
Our tissues are not chosen, we do with them

what we can. The kind domestic gentleman
    contains this killer whom he covers up and
cares for in his dreams. But once
                        last winter,
walking the a.m. dark through ice-fog,
he felt his cage come open, having reached

    a new design remoteness, fog and freeze were
part of—a clean escape from
                        wanting too much love.
Snow turning gray toward dawn, a thin white cat
crouched on the hood of a truck. He
                        struck a match
    and watched it flare, burn, blacken, die as smoke.

His name is gone,
                        dissolved, and in another season
I wake on the Chena in the red canoe, just as
    the paddle-wheeler
                        named "Discovery II" looms
over us. From three high decks, a lovely white and
    blue, tourists gawk down and wave as Ben waves back.

Then into its sudden wake, we dive and roll.
    Convulsing peaks and troughs we—rocking—
muddle through,
                        together, threatened, contemplating
shore—a sodden swim. Perhaps we'd make it, shaken
    and chilled raw. "Hold on," I shout, "stay low!"

My pulse begins to slow, and now my Polish
    grandmother hovers over this. A great dark shape
when I was four, she carried
                    me out and
dropped me seething in. I felt my panic grow
    beneath the Atlantic's
                    salt and spit, unlikely fish,

flapping toward sandy ground. As everything falls
crisply to its spot, the river,
                  calming, brings in focus
    all my obstinate shores. In mid-career, the heart
tempers its beat, you switch from beef to fowl,
    from anger to a gentler disaffection. Now, if ever,

you must catch your early purpose, stitch it to
    your chest like a tattoo. The mast, the manatee,
the mutineer become
                your emblems—those images of
water and the past. The branch of a skinny aspen
    floating by, Jeffrey leans halfway out and hauls

    it in, dousing his brother. Benjamin throws
a fit. I shift him to my seat,
                stand, stretch,
sit, and, starting to lie back…almost before I see
    it go—what might have been a fish, caught
in the shore-weeds, branches, belly up. I thought

I glimpsed a face, white, bloated, bobbing past.
    A blood-drained salmon floating in a pool?
The look and smell of fish. Or—was it?—an
                old drunk,
lost, who stumbled in and drowned, got carried from
    downtown to where the Chena bends, and found

the shore, snagged in a sweeper, resting on his back.
    Time stipples, bubbles, fizzes.
                                 I tell myself,
      that old man was a fish, and then dismiss
the thought, knowing
                    I'll worry later what I've done.

Breaking apart, you gather up the shards of your
decay and puzzle till an
                  edge defines its match,
    paddle till your shoulders take on paddling
as their mission
              and reward you with a piece of self.

The river swinging south, sweepers brush by.
    Against a longer view, Mt. Deborah and Mt. Hess,
white breasts among the clouds, appear and
disappear, and then another,
                 greater river
    plucks us like a twig and sweeps us west.

A spinning fish-wheel passes quickly. Speed
lifts us out of torpor. "Watch out, sit and be still!"
    Nancy alerts the kids. The Tanana means business.
Its glacial grit
             abrades the hull. The surface
like a horizontal curtain in the wind, knotted

then smooth, then flexing like the muscles of
    a gray young body dancing. I clutch a kicking paddle
and my knuckles hum.
               We sight on a sandy spit
where tents and motorhomes sit toylike, dogs and
    children scamper. The river,
                sectioned, eddies,

flows, dead spots a darker gray, and far as the eye
goes west, the sun leans on an elbow big enough
to drink the river up.
                              Above, five wavering
gulls; ahead, a green flat-bottomed airboat
    blasting hard against the current. Black stunted

spruce on the flats, gray hills, and whiteness
    in the range. A sudden
                              happiness in things
that pins us to this place. The house we've built
appears above us, shapely
                              on its ridge, as the airboat,

splashing, cuts
              across our bow, and giddily
    we're doused and shouting at the long end of
this alabaster day. The afternoon,
                              not fragments,
finally, but sitting still and moving in the mind

of this old badger, or like some northern crockery
    with fireweed for border. And pulling in to shore—
a yard, a car on blocks, refrigerator
                              rusting on its side—
    this quiet moment looking down through silt:
one orange stone and countless petals of light.

III

ELISABETH VIGÉE-LEBRUN: SELF-PORTRAIT

A peasant hat set back, long hair let down—
and for five minutes at a time your

eyes are held by mine, and by my lips'
slight part. I practiced an art

without shadows, each pigment in a brighter mode,
and I looked as good as my portraits

in those days. How fine
to have a wife so gifted, pretty, smart,

but he abused my art
and gambled the money away. I hid

the jewels. But when he ruffled me one time
too many I packed my case

and made my way to court,
a life I might have sunk in

like the goose-down mattress on my bed,
but something in me said

a woman's luck can change.
I had a trade while all the excellence around me

knew only how to ride, to speak, to dance.
I lived to paint,

and even on the morning of my daughter's birth
worked in my studio

between the pains. What joy
to trace their diaphanous hair,

the wistful lace at their wrists.
So few of my paintings please me

fully even now, but you must admit
my blues and pinks are not insipid.

No man could do as much. Few worked
as hard or loved the monarchy as I.

One night I saw my husband at a ball. Laughing,
I removed his wig and wiped

the powder from his blushing face. I put a sheet
around him for a toga, crowned him

with a wreath, a theme
that leapt from court to town, the Greek

age come again. Oh but all the paint
in Paris could not save the queen.

They had a guillotine
for me. I saw one head cut off

and carried on a pike. We fled
by coach that night through the cruel

impoverished streets, and
ate just gruel and bread crust

for the three disordered weeks
we jounced to Italy.

Unlike the ill-tempered wealth
that follows, they were knowledgeable, chic,

and—often—sympathetic, but it took a poet's
art to show what wanted to be seen.

Especially the queen. I loved her,
loved her gentlemen and ladies, who also

lost their heads and I cursed my Roman
comforts in those days of

bloody strife, as the tragic news came in—
one after another of my famous sitters

dead. I'd seen them for all time, not
flattering or false, but

as if in a moment of
surprising natural beauty,

alive today if paint
could heal the razored heartbeats of a life.

"A-CRANBERRYING"

From Thoreau's journal

Though he foresaw "a lame conclusion" to
his walk, he noted that plans you have
low expectations for often surprise you,

since intuition like the vibrant whir of
news on a hummingbird's wing may veer beyond
the commonplace—as at the modest shack

he'd built beside the not-yet-famous pond
just a short stroll down the Fitchburg track
from home. So putting his politic worries

to one side, he departs his usual sphere,
crosses Great Field to Beck Stow's swamp, where,
to his delight, large clusters of cranberries

raft like red foam on the sphagnous flood,
removes his shoes and socks and wades into mud.

A RENAISSANCE ALTARPIECE

Uccello painted them: a family bound
together to a tree-trunk post, staring
with horror down as flames leap up from
foot to calf to knee. Four horsemen on
the right display the flag of Rome. Across
from them, with faces glistening in the flame-
light, stand the helmeted guards who
trussed this family up and set them blazing.

Two boys, both red-heads, share their parents'
fate, while in the background—fields, a leafy
apple tree, farm houses, and a church.
The sky behind a neighbor castle town
is black. The merchant and his pregnant wife
and boys were damned for what they did to
desecrate the host. "Religion," I once
told a Catholic friend, "makes good people better,

bad people worse." Another panel illustrates
their crime. They cooked it in a pan until
it bled. The blood of Christ spilled out and ran
across the floor, and when it dribbled
underneath the door, they were exposed.
Have you ever fallen from the second
story window of a dream—the broken
glass, the silent floating scream? You'd think

at least the child in her womb could be
redeemed. Why would a Jewish merchant
be so hostile to the host? Why in
Urbino was this credited? What calculus
of feeling can elucidate this art, unless
it charts a program to annihilate
a race. Aghast, the baffled victims
stare at lizard flames that leap and leap.

COUNTING CARIBOU—PRUDHOE BAY, ALASKA

after R. Glendon Brunk

Tundra to the horizon peppered with lakes,
aswim with pintails and loons. A fox lopes by.
The sky's aslant with jaegers, rough-legged hawks.
I'm paid to tally caribou, a science guy.

Behind me a maze of pipes, pumps, drill-
pads, gravel pits, and sludge-smudged drums,
and everywhere the reek of corporate oil.
But hey, I'm here to count the herd, which comes

(if they come at all) too fast to count, then mill
when they hit the pipe. They mass and twitch, until
one coast-bound leader steps up, lifts her muzzle,
sniffs, while baffled calves and mothers nuzzle,
just as a truck roars by, blaring its god-
damn horn and they stampede away. I hate this job!

ABOVE THE TANANA: FOR JERRY CABLE

1. APRIL, 1988

I squint into the morning's brilliance—
sun on ice at sixty degrees warm. Beyond

the ledge the river holds its form,
but you have left us for some grimmer place.

The other day I thought I saw your face.
At the wheel of a pick-up you pulled out of

the Pumphouse heading home. I know the mind
can play such tricks, unwilling or unable

to let go. Behind me, Spirit's pawing the dry
leaves. I hear her collar jingle but keep mum.

Out of the west two Phantom bombers come:
like tandem wasps they home in on their base.

Mt. Hayes is hazy, Deborah lost in clouds.
I summon back your dying year of verse,

no loss of power in its quirky grace. Then Martha's
whispered message on the phone: "It won't be long."

We saw the lights one midnight from your place,
a lovely sky-show—blooms and tendrils

constantly born and dying out in space—
whose abstract beauty served to keep us warm.

No flowers yet, no sap smell from the trees.
Crossing the ice—the giant shadow of a bird.

I look into the sun, seeking its source.
My eyes go liquid and my mind goes numb.

2. ONE YEAR LATER

A second winter plays out its strong hand.
Jerry—as pain grows less and bitter knowledge

more, I can't forget you in your dying year—
the bold words coming as your drugs allowed

their odd, particular humor, their angular warmth.
A six dog sled, when I arrived through drifts

at this clear, rooted spot, was loping by.
Watching their avid speed, I thought about

your progress into dust—what part of air
you are. What other shore has your increase

of wisdom in decay released you to? Near tundra
yesterday, I drove northeast from town; a raven and

a rough-legged hawk fought on the road. The silver
bird flew up and hovered, while the dark one

hopped and fluttered into brush. At 3 a.m. a bloody
wash lacquered the southern sky. I felt complicit

with its morbid chemistry. Perhaps it's just
the vanity of art that rips through muscle

to expose the heart? You knew such qualms.
Those dogs looked happy in the brilliant haze.

The driver was absorbed by her soft ride.
Pulled by my words, I follow into wish—

a rune, a riddle some lost persona utters
that will not be forgotten in the rush

of what we are into what
isn't us and couldn't care.

3. A SECOND YEAR

The brown leaves rattle on a cottonwood.
No crocuses, no rose buds, but the snow

begins to vacate this secluded spot,
and sun sparks through the spruce. Jerry,

last night at a banquet in your honor
as you sat across from me, silent while

purple phrases bloomed into bright porphyry
that surely would have faded on the page,

when my turn came no words occurred.
Could silence honor you like poetry?

At least you were still living in my dream.
Awake, I know you're buried in your home county,

but we can talk. Indulge my fantasy.
I'd like to fill you in. Those Russian verbs

you sweated might prove useful after all,
with Eastern Europe under democratic rule

and Bering Strait these days quite crossable.
You know about the killings in the Sound,

dead birds, sea otters, seals, dead everything.
You shake your head in fury and your sickened

face turns red. I hear you crying, "Shit
on Alyeska!" for the spill. You worked

the arctic slope and know those
creeps would stop at nothing to make dough.

A mottled gray on white of passing clouds
flows on the ice. Our friends agree that

you still hang around, part of the air,
part of the supple ground. At least what's

in me doesn't ache as much, though there's an absence
like an organ that's been cut. Another

season's passing and I need to keep in touch.

4. STILL REMEMBERING

A greening jasper in the slough as water
pushes up. The hillside's sage—

I pluck a sprig, rub it between
my fingers for its aromatic breath

recalling the teas you kept
in packs—Earl Grey and Lapsang—scattered

around your place the year when you lived humbly
in a one room shack on a downtown Fairbanks street

and Martha studied out of state. I'd cycle
by to visit, drink your bourbon, share

your tapes of poets, exchange views. Does James
Wright's work go sentimental in the end?

You said it was too easy to get drunk
at the Dog or the Boatel, the local dives,

and come back stinking, flushed, needing
to straighten out and write. You'd crash

the whole next day. Thank god for poetry,
you said, to keep us sane. I stop and wonder,

am I crazy to go on with you like this?
Say it: he's dead, and nothing could be worse.

But as I rise to go a raven flashes up croa-
croaking from the island just off-shore.

He yells and circles, dives, swings by, and
floats on down the slough, then turns again—

a black hole on the sky that whirls me
in its almost human eye, a voice

as desperate and playful as your verse.

ASK LOUISE

Even the love letters disappoint—
too innocent and dear amid
their dust and one cent stamps.
From the heart of Indiana
with Louise, you brought them back

and at your sister's house we unpack
cartons, read their faded hands.
This formalized regret for 'Sam,'
a son now dead no matter what:
"may scripture give thee comfort."

Timid Louise—surprise—had bought a Dodge
and taught herself to drive at sixty-five.
And this from New Orleans—"We've
few Friends here, thy faith is wanting"—
chills me with vast differences. We pass

the sugar tongs and bowl with purple
tarnish hatched two centuries back,
ponder initials on the florid silverware,
and polish a serving spoon to a soft
sheen to glass its curlicues: *A S*.

And these pince-nez—too quaint!
We thumb through photos for the odd
resemblances. Whose riding camp was this
with distant cousins caught
in happy genteel pre-war poses

too stiff to be believed? Or else—
let's ask Louise. I wonder will they
box our things like this, toss most,
and salvage what holds value
in an age when overcrowding's certain,

winter doubtful. Is longevity assured?
Last week Louise, our link, moved
to a home. She can't depose the evidence
we've plundered. Phew—pink polish stinks.
Shaky with absences we pack it up.

INTO MY HEAD

after Frigyes Karinthy

A squeal of bit on bone that opens up
the skull. A sucking sound as liquids drain
from ventricles, linked lakes inside the brain.
Strapped on my stomach to the tabletop,

I seem to rise above him, float apart,
and watch him lift cracked bones out with gloved hands,
then split the lobes and stare, while I assess his art.
He palms the insidious fruit with crimson strands

twining around, a curse, an adverse jewel
growing inside, which brings on nonstop night
and the clatter of trains that rattle me out of
myself until I hardly know what's real.
He bites his lip and lops the canker out.
"Cheer up, old mole," he says. "With luck you'll live."

TWO VIEWS OF THE WRECKAGE

for the artist, Kes Woodward

[Note: Climate change models show interior Alaska
becoming dryer while coastal areas flood worldwide.]

Kibitzing over your shoulder as you
sketch those billowing clouds above the
staved-in houseboat in its dried up slough,
I sense the berrying bear that ambled by a
day or two ago leaving this gritty substance,
fear, like a pheromone, hanging there
and there—and because we codgers share
a wish to buck the laws of change and chance

you cache the present scene while I flash on
distant glittering Venice seen back when
the band played gaudy Liszt and Beethoven
and Sputnik shimmered over St Mark's Square
where now high waters climb the palace stair
as ice-sheets thaw and toxic tides roll in.

SOUNDS IN A FOREST

Between the inlet and the gated homes,
this bike path—muddy, tree-shadowed, with
the heavy scent of loam—while off to our left
a great blue heron perches on a rock, and
overhead Ben spots an osprey nest. He rides
a yellow three-wheeled Terratrike, low
to the ground in case a seizure strikes.

Then as we circle back a splitting sound
sharp as a whip-crack splinters through the woods
where maples, oaks, and chestnuts arch, and then
a stairstep stutter, "cra…cra…craa…craa…craa"
like something big's about to fall on us.
Are we the butt of nature's sly retort
to Berkeley's two-faced riddle of design?

And in that moment's indecision—
should we flee or wait out the conclusion,
the way things happen in the *now*—a child's
sickness or a parent's passing, buildings charred
to rubble, planes gone down—who's left to say,
if a big-leaf maple tree uproots and
lands on top of us, what sound occurred?

Philosophy is empty here. A nest's sweet
fissure where the eggs were laid, a slug's
retreat, a squirrel's stomping ground may
come to grief, as I recall my last night's dream—
in a flooding house, we hurried up the stairs
and saw through gutted roof the clouds
like spigots pouring inspiration down.

And then it happens—an object sonorous
with leaves slapping past leaves, its bark rasping
past other limbs, and all those minor intricate lives
dependent on that branch, flummoxed,
must pack up and move to other digs
as all my stale beliefs come floating like
a cancelled midnight stanza from the sky.

AMERICAN TALIBAN

Because of divorce he sought
wholeness, because of affluence,
poverty. Inflexible diversity
drove him toward uniformity,
though if he'd been truly violent,
he'd have put on a uniform.

Drawn to his local mosque
by the flatteries of prayer,
he fell on his knees toward Mecca,
and took up a new fidelity,
then making his way to Yemen,
joined in an antique reading

of the text, which speeds from
the Prophet's hand straight to
the eyes and heart of man. As hair
and beard grew wild, he mixed with
the sons of tribesmen, no longer
a skittish child, and girded himself

to fight. We saw him the other night,
carried from the cellar of the bloody
Afghan fortress and met our own
confusion in his swooning,
sleepless eyes, but hidden in their
wounded animation, cocked grenades

beneath a turban, were the fateful
words of Allah, merging camels
and commotion, the Covenant and
Gospels, donkeys drowned in
swirling waters in the land-locked
land of Omar, doubtful nation,

where devotion haunts the part of
us we squander when we batten
down or knuckle under and
calls upon that goodness which
created us in stages—called by us,
like Noah, *"God-possessed."*

THE ASSIGNMENT: HARVARD, 1962

The sedge has wither'd from the lake
And no birds sing

A gray afternoon. I lay on my
bed, like a gun aimed at a target
with no one to pull the trigger.
There was an ocean with ripples
and waves and an occasional

seabird far in the distance and I
rose and fell with the swell of it,
deep in the belly of not wanting.
So dinnertime passed as I lay there
with the assignment, due the next day,

undone. Hectoring thoughts whirled
through me like hailstones—this was
the end of freedom, the end of
happiness—as the hours passed and
misery lashed me with her whip.

I dozed briefly and lurched
awake with frayed nerves and
clammy skin. It was winter,
bare trees, birds gone south,
and something inside me was broken.

I'd come to the end of childhood
in the grip of a monstrous fear
that I might be turning into someone
I wouldn't even like—some twit,
dull, snotty, bookish, and dry.

Next day, I got up around noon,
splashed water on my face,
dragged myself to my desk, and
did it, and at the very last minute
turned it in. Had anything changed?

Not really. For months after,
I kept looking in on myself like
a nurse on a sickly patient, taking
the weak pulse of my feelings,
fearing a relapse, until one day

I glanced out the window and saw
down in the courtyard the bright
yellow blooms of forsythia
and felt my bruised core mending,
as my heart rattled back to life.

THE UNNAMED LAKE

In memory of Charles Ott and William Ruth, Denali Park photographers

Slogged over tipsy muskeg, past a "moose
wallow," grizzly tracks, to reach this breeze-
rippled lake, where, through waving horsetails,
a golden-eye, her pesky offspring in tow,

preens and dives. Across the sky-flecked water, spruce,
then tundra meadows mount toward jagged Zs
of rock. Like specks of white-out, Dall sheep line
the ridge. If this place had a name, it's been

erased, in homage to two men whose ashes
seed the hills nearby. They staked their lives
on wildness beyond naming. Can we go back,
reclaim the power of unaltered place? Blue
and luminous, a damselfly lights on this page;
two kingfishers weigh in, wheel off down the lake.

DENALI PARK FALL DRIVE-THROUGH

This roadside nature was once
wilderness, which now boasts
campsites, toilets, rangers, rows
of split-log benches by the lake.

By the lake loud honks and squeaks,
a skyey tumult. We look up
where specks by the dozens swirl
like streamers, sink, form rippling Vs,

then lift and vanish into air as
hundreds more, riding the thermals,
circle toward Denali's mass, a
vast white humpback whale set off

by craggy pyramids too tall for
cranes to top. How thrilling,
operatic, this sky teeming with
birds blown in from the lonely tundra

to greet the turning season—a frenzied,
festive, taxis-in-Times-Square
cacophony of cranes! One red capped pair
skims low, long-necked, hooked

beaks like spears with spindly
trailing legs, then catching an
updraft, rise into the sky's blue
brilliance seeking passage through.

PSALM: AFTER NIETZSCHE

That day is coming soon when our people,
all the cousins, pets, children
will begin to disperse like the insects
of summer after the petals fall.
And where do they go, those bees,

those dragonflies? Into the soil
where they break into pieces, a wing,
an antenna, a thorax, absently dreaming
of spring, as the long cold settles over
them, their buzzing and sipping forgotten.

And a great age passes like those
lumbering eras we learned of
in grade school, or the unbelievable time
it takes to make a star and its planets and
evolve a living world—all gone to ground,

and trillions of years slip by in silence
under the earth, but then one day, one
millennium, a gentle humming and something
oozing, gripping, reaching, this relentless longing
toward light—urgent, fantastic. It could happen.

Two Long Poems

THE WEDGE

Alexander Pearce was transported for seven years for
stealing six pairs of shoes. He had arrived in Van Dieman's
Land in 1820. —Robert Hughes, *The Fatal Shore*

Floggings did not impress me, my other
      blisterings omit. One keeper lounged
on the beach, reading a violet note

from home. I thought of my Irish coast
      as raw as this. With black whales passing,
seals on the rocks near shore, I knew

it could happen tonight—snatching a rowboat,
      we'd paddle the inlet, beach it, and
smash the bottom out with an ax.

Thrashing inland through spiky thickets,
      we carried a few days' meat, and Brown's
needleless compass scribbled on cardboard.

At Frenchman's Cap, a twenty mile radius
      of green and rock—vast sky, the ocean
below, netting its wave on wave—I thought

Is there an end to this moment, someone
      is writing out? And moving on, no lines were
straight. Giant trees striking from clefts,

at night we huddled in caves and hardly slept.
      Who said, "Each idea's like a coin—just
flip it and the reverse is also true?"

This island was inverted Ireland, projected
          through the globe upon the darker south.
Its magnetism had a West pole and an East,

by which we steered, as the weather turned
          to gales, to sleet and moaning winds,
and soon our meat had turned a kelly green

you'd rather starve than eat. My shoes,
          colorless couplings, were passing out of
themselves. Brown, the worst walker, a little man—

he fell behind, and cooed that we should
          wait, wait up for him, not leave him
to the Vandemonian wolves. We swore we might.

Somewhere I've read an army's just a gang of
          thieves led off by someone stupid to get killed.
And deamon land's another way the Saxons

skim their crud, allow your investment
          in a personal world. But to me it's the
aspiration, the fiery resolution and

because—you just can't wall it in.
          And so we straggled, scattering, each
aiming where he thought was east.

That night no one could gather wood enough.
          We helped ourselves, each one his own
little fire. And Kennelly made a crack

that turned our heads: "I feel so weak,"
          he said, "I could eat a slice of man."
Next sun-up Greenhill said he'd seen it done.

We quarreled over this—a cunning murder—
          and who could wolf the man-flesh down?
Till Travers said, "It chews like pork."

I brooded over that—such times you get
        so famished thoughts have juice—
'til finally I asked who it should be.

We looked among ourselves and knew
        the wedge that halves the human heart.
Always the same extremist tales. Ashamed,

you write them down, continue scribbling
        but stop signing your name. Someone
said Dalton—he'd been a flogger.

The whisper went around, we waited
        a day and into the next night until
he fell asleep. Greenhill took the ax

and split him. Mat Travers tossed
        his heart and liver on the fire,
snatched them up and ate them

not half warm. That night I fasted,
        pacing between the brutal odors
of edible meat and sensibility—choice

drawn against a backdrop of nervous
        exhaustion, palmy eucalyptus, coy
kangaroos all framed in the window

of a butcher shop I'd seen one
        glancing back in Hobart. Next day
the interminable arguments of hunger won.

It wasn't smooth. Your empty stomach
        doesn't take meat well. I ate him
more than once and we got moving.

Brown fell behind again, a feeble walker,
        he knew what might be on our minds. Kennelly
too dropped back. Soon they were gone,

we heard no more of them. Five brave men
        left, mid-island, with no map. Nameless
mountains, rivers near their source we

plunged through, until one we couldn't ford
        but had to cross or end up tracked down,
carried back to that malignant hole from

which we'd come. You'd make it to your
        chest, but that was all. One further step,
the famished flood would grab you

by the nape, tumble you in its rush.
        Hearts pounding, we backed off. That night
we caught a wombat—first wild meat

we'd chewed. It lent us strength.
        Shouting our giddy fears, our outrageous
loony scorn to die, next morning three of us

bare-chested, took the plunge, and
        splashed across. Safe, we made a chain
and dragged the others over. But now,

soaked through, the wind came after us
        so cold and wet that we could hardly walk.
More mountains and deep thickets, granite

scarps you had to wedge up with your nails
        rubbed raw, your knees scraped bloody,
aping the stretch of fingers with your toes.

Then finally a valley sweet with grass.
        A late October spring was coming on.
It smelt like sugar in a jar you drop

a string through till it crystals.
        We saw some kangaroos too swift to catch,
and camping by a stream, Bodenham slept first

and Greenhill smashed his skull. It was his
       turn to make his way to bones. The rest—
we swore we'd die together as one man.

Oh God, sometimes in dreams I'd see
       your face: you'd sit at your writing desk
gazing at trees whose branches webbed

the sky. Look down—the jagged ink blot
       on your pad, does it suggest my Irish mouth
in flaming execration? Dim children of

an idealistic age, we thought a word
       could mate us, wash away the scars the
stealing of a half a dozen shoes had gouged.

But when the craving comes you don't
       know what you'll do. Three times we almost
killed a kangaroo, but when the ax

bounced off or flew wide, they were gone.
       As Greenhill went to get it, Mather said,
"Who's next? He'd kill his priest

before he'd fast one day." But on that open
       plain we couldn't make our break. He had
the only blade, we'd grown too weak.

Camped by a creek that night, we boiled
       the last of Bodenham, which scarcely
kept our faculties in motion. Mather

could not eat. He cooked some roots
       and scarfed them down, but no one's
stomach could have held that mess.

And while he vomited, Greenhill
       took the ax, snaked up behind him
in the grass, and struck a partial blow.

Mather—in a miracle—jumped up and fought
      till I and Travers joined and pulled him off.
We calmed them down and sat around the fire

in a sicklier despond than I had ever known.
      I saw that Travers was on Greenhill's side,
they'd have their way. I took a stroll

and looking back I watched them collar him.
      He cried out for a Christian death.
As Greenhill raised the ax I turned away.

That site where Mather died we camped
      an extra day, then marched off east,
and he and I and he made fugues around

the forward-backwards counting song—
      "seven little, six little, five little
cannibals." Travers was stinking.

His green foot that a snake had bit
      could barely carry him. He begged us to
go on, abandon him. He claimed what Mather

we had left would take us to a town.
      But Greenhill told him no—we'd stick and
pull him through. Lapsing in and out of fever,

fearing what we'd do, poor Travers couldn't sleep.
      Half dragging and half carrying we moved
him along, exhausting our own strength.

We bore a week of this. Mather was gone.
      And finally when Greenhill bared the ax
Travers in an almost grateful agony

stretched out and gave his life away.
      Now we were two, with summer coming on,
and but for the kangaroos, the country

we strolled through reminded me of home:
        low hills with grass, trees in little
copses on their brows, a mild fruitful

landscape that kept my spirits up.
        Flowers, birds whose names I wish
I'd learned. At night a million stars.

One cross above, another on the ground
        that fed my hope we'd find some sheep,
a settlement, a town—make it to Hobart,

slip onto a returning convict boat, and who
        could say I hadn't served my time? I'd wake
to a council of one, the always affirmative "I."

But Greenhill's down. I think he gloms me more
        than usual. He keeps the ax and says we'll never
make it. I stand apart, and squat only when he does.

Last night across the fire he crooned:
        "I seen a thief cut down and limp across
the prison yard, at every step blood gushing

from his shoes. A spaniel licked the gore
        from the lashing post, a thousand ants
a-scavenging the meat the cat had scattered."

I said I'd seen as bad. He said,
        "The lasher's face was shattered. His
mouth, slashed at an angle, declared

he'd whipped Napoleon and gave no spit
        for whipping us. His right eye, mangled,
stuck out like a crab's. He wore it

as a badge. My time, I never screamed
        till after ninety strokes, and then
there came a groan that wasn't me, and was,

I couldn't hold. It seems he'd
        opened up the spine, and after that, no thing
I wouldn't do. You never live that down."

Then Greenhill raised the ax and held
        it to his head. "You see the man."
I wanted him to do what he was thinking.

I said, "I've seen a child of less than ten,
        whipped into mush." "That's justice sure,"
he laughed. "The world be damned."

We weren't closer for the talk. I knew
        that he was ill-disposed toward me.
We sat across the fire. I heard a

croaking bird, the wash of wind in grass,
        the goat-skin that was thudding
in my heart. Toward dawn he fell asleep.

I took the ax from underneath
        his head and sank it in his skull. My
body spasmed at the crack and jism came.

I took his shoes, then cooked a leg,
        ate, slept, and had another dream. It was
the virgin mother aging in my arms. I hugged

her close but she went slack and died.
        The worst thing sometimes happens, was my
thought on waking up. I made his pants

a sack and, bagging several tender
        parts, moved on. Some native black men
helped me once, then ran. I found a river,

followed to a farm. I'm not afraid
        to name the dead. They're no part of me now.
Evaporation is their home. And stepping

over bony ground—this land where time
　　is portioned out in absences—my mind is
ready to accept the ends that disable

and dissolve and form beyond our knowing.
　　Tell that I'm ready to take the cure
—just let's not talk about sauces.

You say 'no' to your name, and walk out,
　　feeling the sun at your back.
Yesterday's seeming cracks and drips

to the ground, and you aren't terrific,
　　just mild, your face in chalk on
the pavement. In infamy they say we're

all alike. The shoes—I smell them
　　every time I think of meat. If that's
my fate, well I can live with it.

* * *

RIVER OF LIGHT: A CONVERSATION WITH KABIR

Introduction

River of Light: A Conversation with Kabir takes the reader on a week-long raft trip down a wild river in southcentral Alaska. Bears, eagles, moose, seals, otters and salmon inhabit the poem's world, and the river's shifting landscape of glaciers, mountains, rapids, and waterfalls energizes its meditative mood. The trip becomes a spiritual journey as well, since the poem includes commentary by the 15th century Indian mystic poet Kabir (pronounced *kuh-BEER*), who serves as a kind of mentor for the poem's narrator. Kabir often speaks in riddles, but his core teaching is clear: organized religions are useless, and spiritual truth can only be found by looking inside yourself. The raft trip described in the poem took place in 2003, the year of the second Iraq War, so the war is on the narrator's mind and becomes a metaphor for his inner struggles. But the main story of the poem is the trip itself, as the river's waves and currents influence the shaping and pacing of its lines, and the wildlife and scenery provide frequent surprises for the travelers.

PROLOGUE: CHITINA, ALASKA, JULY 2003

We met in a garden of bones, behind
an abandoned church—disheveled
                                      and dated
stones with fragments of muscular saints
from a past
                 that had lost its way.

A party of pilgrims preparing to float,
the river rippled behind us
            beyond the caribou mask,
while petals of expectation settled
            around the benches like
a snowfall of ancient wisdom
                      melting into mud.

My plate stained with moose stew
                                      and chili,
his maxims burdened my backpack which
pinched, so I shrugged it off.

They evoked an inscrutable journey
      like the drift out of sight of
a bevy of swans
          that you peer at till
nothing is left. Elsewhere

the war continued.
          It wasn't
the cure we'd expected, and it
doused our initiation into
        the sect that danced
in my dream underwater, all their clothes
left behind
      beside the plaque that
   clattered from
         the wall with these
words by Kabir: *Better think twice*
before you hang with someone like me.

I. THE THREE WORLDS

And so I unpacked my gear
which held just a wet-bag and
tent. Camped
      beside the river, the swish
of a fishwheel lulling, I sifted through
his weavings
      whose riddles wooed me to sleep.

Tomorrow the rafts will take us
wherever the
      current threads.
I can only aid with my paddle,
and hope that our skipper can steer.

Be passive before your fate,
the generalissimo croons, be
         strong

when the winds of fire
send shrapnel around your ears.
Listen, says Kabir, *I have a*
humble request. I'm locked in this
jailhouse for life, please
                    toss me the key.

Odysseus rides in one raft—
a hound with a flea-bitten ear—
and once we
                pass under the bridge
and wave the dip-netters good-bye
forsaking our lap-tops and
                            cell-phones,
our links to the world
                    disappear. *All*
Creation began, notes Kabir,
at one single point. And no one
can say where it's going.

The mountains behind us shrink
back. The walls of the canyon
move in while sun
                    sparks the ripples
to flame. Here in the land of
no night, the
                answers we seek
cache their names, or as sage Kabir
warns, *The ones who scrambled*
                        for life-boats
            drowned in mid-river.
Only their wetsuits survived.

Where space is at war with darkness
tanks move in throwing flames.
Our temple's knocked down,
                            their mosque
chopped up like pâté. Whose statue

stood in the square,
                    whose divisions
contesting the rule of our rational precepts
empurpled the sky? A widow in
mourning beside her husband's body.
A child in tears.
                    The three worlds are
simply a trap, says Kabir,
when death is on the march.

II. THE COSMIC BEAST

Over the clouds the air thins,
a contrail crosses
                    the sky
and the moon is as faint as this page.
I'm lost in the strangeness of travel,
unsure
            what my duties will be.
All the rails have been
taken away that brought
the hard wealth from
                    the mines,
smelted down to make steel for
our wars. I open my inward eye
and guess where these channels may lead.

When a sudden squall splutters and
spits, the river
                    spits back at the sky.
A loon by the bank, flaps spray and
gulps down a fish. We move
without push or
                    pull on the back
of the seasonal melt that rocks us placidly
like a camel plodding the dunes.
All the streams that flow into
the Ganges, become the Ganges, he says.

And I feel a wildness inside,
a diaphanous
            dislocation, as my soul
reaches out toward the heights
where the moon finds a new
vantage point, winking
                        over the western
rim. *Having slept for millions of years,*
Kabir asks, *isn't it time to wake up?*

What brachiation means
we can no longer do.
                        The jungle
gym of this world has mostly rusted
away and moved inside where we live.
In this cave that we
                        heat with old tires
and paint with ancestral ash
like the cave-dwelling apes
we once were, we
                carry the load
of our past and burden
ourselves like tame beasts.

When it's time to pull in for
the night, the river's a mighty
arm. We paddle like mad toward
shore but are
                carried beyond
the point. "All out!" our skipper
yells and we jump in the
shallows
            and pull, slog,
                        splash, shiver
and shout. We are gods of the river
at last as we haul the raft onto a bar.

Looking ahead through the eons, one

galaxy intersects ours but the rest fly
off into
   space. And space and
        time
are unstable, like a drunken elephant
wild-eyed, dashing with swaying trunk,
         and we're
carried along on its back. *Your mind
is a cosmic beast*, he observes,
that rushes away to the end.

III. A MUSE

Happy her name and her fate,
a great aunt who circled
    the world, but
somehow missed India, his country
shaped like a heart. Living to109,
she smoked and
    drank till the end
and died peacefully in
her sleep. We honor her daring and charm.
*If you don't break
    those ropes
when alive*, says Kabir, *will your
ghost do it after you're dead?*

The moon and sun have gone
down, but light comes from
a thousand directions
    and washes
over my tent as the creatures
of night awaken. A brown bear
swims toward this island smelling
our human detritus,
    the sweetness of
toothpaste, of bourbon. What use
are such things in the wild? I

heave them into
                    the current, watch
as the danger recedes. *Spotting*
a four footed creature, the hunter
took off, notes Kabir, *although*
that celestial beast might well
            have defanged his fear.

                    *

Not very far from here, seven kids
on wilderness training,
                    prepared to
cross a stream when out of the willow
brush a sow grizzly charged. One's leg
is ripped
            open, ribs broken, a
lung is pierced. Too sudden for
pepper spray or
                    gun, when
she looms up your instinct yells
Run! Big
            mistake.

The sound of the river receding,
a spider
            crawls over my tent. Its threats
web
        into my waking. Inside
its weavings, I ask, What is
my death to you?
                    Where is a place that
will make the soul less thirsty? he asks.
But I'm just fine where I am.
                    Spare me the trip.

                    *

By morning we roll up our tents.
A raven

cackles, "Hello." The channel's
a maze of distractions. It smells like
a peppery absinth,
                    flitting over the landscape
like small birds who have
                    nowhere to hide.

We're latter-day explorers. Coming
after the gold has been
                    staked, we
dig for copper and tin and barter
our grub for fool's gold. On the river
we banter and joke. This
                    float's a
diversion from labor and hints at what
may come after. *Why waste your time*
digging for riches? he asks. *Man's life is*
    a column in chalk that
                    adds up to zero.

IV. AMID MUCUS AND BLOOD

A lightning bolt followed by thunder.
Odysseus hulks under a blanket.
Harsh rain brings a chill to
                    the river.
We put on our ponchos and gloves.
Near shore, among islets we paddle,
pursuing a rushing sound
                    that begins
higher up
        in the mountains,
like something you lost long
ago, and trickles
                    down the rocks—
fresh water to top off our jugs.

How the strange becomes familiar,

like the cries of
                  the next-door
children when it's time for their naps.
This breeze has a roughness like
spruce-bark and the green of mosses
and ferns, verdant
                  sparks in a slow-
moving current, not just one but
a thousand referrals to a past
that can't be undone. *How is it*
I got so old, Kabir asks,
while no one was looking?

The tasks we can manage
are small ones. Put them aside, let
the tatters of fragments of
meanings sculpt a wish-list bones
couldn't foresee. Design
                        is inherently
random, a balance that almost
happens. The first touching of bodies
in marriage can never be
properly planned. *We begin amid*
mucus and blood, says Kabir,
and that's how our story ends.

                *

Wind's up and a copter drops down
with a sudden *thwop thwop* of blades
as it
      lashes the tent flaps. I blink into
dusky midnight where
                        it squats above
the river. 'Someone is terribly
damaged!' I brood, and
                  toss the whole night
as its rotors rattle my dreaming.
And still at breakfast I stew,

that creepy dragonfly-buzz, like a saw
cutting through me—I can't
                         shake it off.
It brings back the lost summer when,
trekking a southwest butte, I
                         wandered from
the trail. Stuck on a sandstone ledge,
I remember starting to slip.
                         Skull cracked, face
           crusted, front teeth gone—
a chopper bore
           me to safety, a rescue I
  have no
           recall of, because I wasn't awake.
Just look around, says Kabir. *See this world
for what it is: a foolish bag of tricks.*

V. NOT CHEAP

Sun jackknifes into
                    the river. Elsewhere,
wars blight and innocents die. The tyrant's stash
of weapons
              has gone missing: what happens
a world away can snowball and ricochet
                         and find us here.

       The river's texture of fish-skin,
sparks, and
              burbles breeds a harvest
of grief. The month my
                    mother died,
I plied her with chocolate
determined to
              keep her alive. Near the end,
I touched a damp sponge to
                         her lips, then
squirted some morphine in to soften

the ache as her vital organs
                              shut down.
How shallow her
                      breathing. I offered
her orange juice, tilting the glass
and she whispered, "More," then
                                    "More!"—
her last words
              that echo in me
                              now. *My whole life*
was a dream, he declares,
and by god I slept right through it!

                *

In no hurry, our patched rafts glide with
the river, drifting from
                          side to side.
We can see a gash where boulders
rolled down
              the hill, and behind it
glimpse mountains
                      fractured in
last year's quake. For ninety seconds
rattled, rocked
          then jolted and jerked, books

falling from
              shelves, and
          crockery smashed, while
                      out here a lake
          broke through its natural
dam and acres of water drained off.
This solid earth we
                  tread on, says Kabir,
is founded on chaos—
one slip and a thousand drown.

We pull in and make camp

early, pack
                a sandwich and climb
to a wider view.
                        A friend opens
his sketchpad and I watch the clouds
take shape—some
                        wisps high up, then
        solider cumulous drifting
over a mountain's hanging glacier
textured like sheep's wool. Below it
the river's gray, streaked
                                with pink, cyan,
        chartreuse. "The colors in nature,"
he tells me, "are never
                        just one thing."

Such a delicate machine, Kabir
observes: *The mind is like a tree
with its roots in the sky
                        and branches
underground.* In those branches moles
are singing and
                        the half moon hangs.
Holding my breath, I
                        can hear the hum
of the river, the pulsing of blood in my ears,
while the hand
                        that colors this landscape
whispers its cadence to paper.
                                I recall to
my artist friend
                        how driving to our launch point
a creature
                        trotted across the road. Long snout
and scrawny tail, it was neither
fox nor dog.
                "A wolf?" he asks, but it
was not a wolf.

"A wolverine?" I shake
my head, then ask if I can
buy his sketch. "I'll have to
                        touch it
up back home." He grins. "They
                aren't cheap, you know."

VI. WANTON WISH

Some seed a mother planted? Some
wanton wish anchored
                    to hope, one paints,
another writes,
                the way some other kid
might fall for racing cars and probing under
the hood take up an unseen life, an
                            inner one,
and decades later haul his ass
around a muddy track or
sweat his time out in a grunge garage.
Put the bit in its mouth, says Kabir,
a saddle on
        its back and ride your
runaway mind all the way to paradise!

Down at the bank where riffles
                            soften,
current spins
            we place our nets, then
stack up drifted logs and set them blazing.
Two pickers
            unpack their guitars
while patience lures our dinner to the net.
I clap my hands and sing, Kabir
declares,
        of the good times and the bad!

Full of fatigue I sleep, but far from

the war I dream of war, as troops
roll into Baghdad throwing flames, planes
strafe a busy street.
                    The inner world
is not so innocent. Born into war,
black headlines blazed the bombings in
Japan before I could
                    read or anyone
explain. *Oh, friend,* Kabir observes,
when you pack a loaded
            gun inside your brain,
how can you ever find the peaceful path?

Next morning—paw prints larger
than my hand. Each digit shows
a claw. We follow,
                    awed by what
has passed our way, down to
a braided stream
                    wade into it, and
stepping
            rock to rock, pick up some
further tracks on the
                    far side. Our skipper
says, "A young one on the move."
Nobody saw or heard it in the night.
And I relate how in Yosemite
a black bear
            mauled some outdoor
sleepers once, while clueless in our tent
we slept right through.

            *

The river widens, mountains
backing off. A young bald eagle,
watches from
            a branch beside a steep
        embankment where

155

the current swerving
                    undercuts the rock—
pebbles and sand break loose,
sliding in glitters of
                    mica, sparks of
ruby, silver-blue and green. We paddle
backwards, hold
                    our place and gaze
          as to our left another
cache spills down
                    with a delicious
sound like
                    bells—entrancing like a piece
for gamelan. Amazing how this cliff
is opening itself, giving
                         its wealth away
perpetually to no one
                    when no one
is here, but now to us. *How wonderful
my luck is*, says Kabir, *my god
                    caresses me
with tenderness that never ends!*

That nature can
                    astonish or appall
means nothing till you
                    grasp it
with your senses, pump it through your heart.
*If you haven't lived
                    through something,*
Kabir notes, *why then it isn't true.*

One time in a gale that whipped
Point Reyes' Light,
                    barreling in
so fiercely that I felt I might
                              just
lean back into it and let that stiff

breeze hold me up,
I found it wasn't easy to give in,
to tilt back and
              submit, putting
my faith in that wind—like trusting
a lover's
              arms and falling back
into this shifty world's profane embrace.

VII. A GOD-LIKE FLAME

For days, we'd seen no human face
but ours but now the water parts
on a
              whiskered face, wide-eyed
and slickly furred,
                            who's trailed the
run of salmon to this joining. It stares
right back at us, dives
                            under, splashes
up on the other side. What's it like
to be a thing of water and find
direction in
              the current's drift,
to delve in deep philosophies
                            of summer fish?
Although you cannot see it, says
Kabir, *a god-like flame infuses every
creature. That's what I'm here to say.*

We beach our rafts. Just sand,
for miles, sand
              more ancient than
these glaciers, a Sahara from another age.
We tromp across
              its face, a wizened
foreign legion of the north. High up,
a raven's heading somewhere else.

The shells we pick up on
                this beach
have turned to stone. This wood
won't burn. Our shadows
                  shimmer
in the antique air. *Those Chinese poets, friend,*
Kabir inquires, *the ones you so esteem, tell me*
did they ever learn
             to walk on fire?

Odysseus rolls
             ecstatic in sand, then
shakes it off like water, wagging
his whole
           body, tail to nose.
His ears perk and he grins
a knowing grin, then licks
his burning paws. So much
                of this
dog's life, he seems to say, is like
old legends scribbled in the sand. You
better get your
             licks in while you can.

Our planet's a tight circle of design,
inside six wider
                circuits and on the next
one out his cousin Rovers sniff for
foreign strains.
           This world, Kabir
reminds us, *with its elephants and*
bedbugs, butterflies and tigers,
                all springs
out of one word and everything
inside that word is full of light.

Past midnight ghostly acolytes
                invade my

tent. Taking my hands, they draw me where
a slow stream pausing
                              widens to a pond,
the whole crew gathered
                              at its edge. What little
we have on we
                    strip away. Can you
escape the chill of history without
protective clothes? There is
                              no other way.

Our former plans,
                    jobs, families dissolve
        like prints of childhood memories
washed out.
                    Naked in summer's twilight
                              we laugh and
wave our arms and
                              chanting spin like
        dervishes, as ice-fire takes
                              our limbs.
We shout
        and splash, breasts
                              sway and cocks
distend. Rocked
                    to a higher plane, we leap
and dash about.
                    Who thought
                              the night could
ever be this bright?
                    Fantastic! Kabir cries. *Don't*
ever let
        a chance like this slip by!

VIII. THE BREATH INSIDE THE BREATH

Next day the river
                    narrows between

159

crags. We hang back, paddling to the side,
and watch three grizzlies
                              prowl their
ledges, time the salmons' leaps and
catch one in
                    their jaws, then
                              drag the flopping
                                        fish away to strip
its flesh.
            But listen, says Kabir, *the answers*
      that you seek are neither East
                              nor West
      and like those fish one day
                  you'll be picked clean.

One scrawny mother with a lame
hind foot prowls our side so close
            her bear-smell and
                        the scraping of her teeth
inflame our senses with essential bear.

The world that we've been given
keeps unfolding into
                        wider facets
and no eagle can see farther than
the mind. We part the
                        final curtain
which opens on
                  an attic full of bats, a sinkhole, a
crevasse from which there is no
climbing out.
            But just look up—those
farther starfields
                  glisten on
                        all sides. *Forget*
the sacred texts, Kabir instructs.
No book is holier than what you read inside.

When finally the grizzlies drift
    away, we make our run.

The river quickens, plunging through
a gap with
    riffles, whitecaps,
whirlpools, church-size rocks. Our skipper
steers us left, but the raft, defiant,
wanders,
    spins. Fighting with paddles,
shouts, as a panicked
    swirling shunts us through

the cleft between
    one hellish rock
and that sheer cliff—and suddenly, I'm in
      the sky,
then under, battling
    in the eddy's drum and
thunder, dragged down,
    and then
      spewed upward,
Maytagged in the clatter,
    rack and din
      of the cycle's
rinsing spin.
    Whirled gasping to the surface—

sucked back in! Friend prophet, have you
any words for me
    in my distress? Kabir
replies: *There are no travelers on*
the river, no ropes, no one to pull.
The breath inside the breath
    is all there is.

Strength sapped by cold, I gurgle
to the surface, belch

                out water, head
reeling past all speaking as
                    the raft
pulls up beside me, offering
a paddle which I cling to, gasping,
as my fellow rafters drag
                    me out. Doused,
chilled—giddy pints of water
                    bolt my
stomach—laughing, tearing,
                    gagging,
as I strain to suck air in.

That river you rafted once, remember,
like a rope frayed at one end
                    you
shimmied down, and where it breaks
apart the
                inside maze has been
                      transformed.
Whoever drinks that liquor, says Kabir,
wanders this world forever like a man insane.

IX. AMAZING THINGS

We drift, then paddle as the current
ebbs, the river broadens, opens
on vast
        sky, a mile wide face
of glacier to our left. The gunshot crack
of icebergs calving
                echoes down
the lake. Bergs drift
                around us, sharks
and great blue whales of ice. "Just look
around"—our skipper's arms sweep wide—
"I call this place
                'the center of the world.'"

We pull up
          on a bar, have lunch and,
basking, take it in,
                    then gather
          by some driftwood, pose and mug.
I have the photo tacked above me here.

The one beside it goes back forty years
and shows the hot-shot poets
                         we once were—
meaning that we knew
                    nothing but had
a way with words and felt they
could sustain
               us through a life. Posed
before a wagon
               and a barn, our master
                    christens us with
bottled beer. And there I am. Scoping
the sky with
               telescopic stick, I grin.
Now half of us are gone.
               This old world, notes Kabir,
is nothing but a gamblers' den
and neither prayers
                    nor cash can
save you when death has you by the balls.

A lake requires rowing so we row
through drifting ice two miles
                         to the shore.
Above its bank, our target bench is
guarded by a single sleeping bear.
We shout and bang on
                    cans. We're
like a Viking raiding party with
our paddle

spears. Long-legged, the
drowsy black bear, rouses, shakes his head
and trudges off, but at
                    a nearby snow patch
settles down
            again and spreads himself, a
sumptuous bear rug. He's past the nuisance
range of shouting but it's not
                        safe to share
the camp.
        Oh friend, wake up! Kabir implores.
The night is over—why
                do you go on sleeping?

Dreaming of some hollow when the
land was dark, a darkness with
a mother's tongue
                rough on his
infant fur. Bear breath
                    a comfort
in the night, while overhead
the constellations
                turn, and
seven brilliant stars shine like a bear.
"Is it the fear of death?" I ask a rafting
friend who
            writes obsessively on bears.
"The opposite," she says. "Bears
are so incredibly alive!"

At last the shifting breeze
                        brings him
our scent, obnoxious
                    to his nose. He rises,
shakes himself and lumbers off. We
occupy the bench. *I've seen*
amazing things, Kabir declares. *A lion*
keeping watch over pastured cows,

                              a mouse chasing
a camel, a son who gave birth to
                        his mother. Friend, when
  you crave an answer
                        this verse is all you need.
"Kabir, you saintly joker," I protest, "these
riddles give scant comfort when we bleed."

X. A RIVER OF LIGHT

An outhouse and a dumpster mark
an end to wilderness. Icebergs from
the glacier, ridged and
                        rutted, filter
and refract the evening light. We form
a circle linking
                    arms and sing "O careless
  love," and
              "Study war no more."
                                New calvings
rumble as the fire dies. As sage Kabir
insists: *Where is authentic wilderness,*
if not
        inside yourself?
                    Something
planted in us is the seed. Everything
                    grows from it,
even the upside-down tree which bears
this poem's fruit.

                    That night,
he scouts me dribbling on a court. I wheel
and deftly pass between my legs.
But when my final
                jump shot hits
the rim and bounds away, he shakes
his head and laughs. *Life's*
                a giddy circus.

Don't forget, wise men and pundits,
                              they're
the biggest fools. This world has ended
many times before.

    I wake up in the silence, stunned.

     *

Last day, we set off rowing down the lake and
drift beneath a great steel bridge, four
spans across, but
                    one of them is down.

Beyond it stands a rippling
                              cliff of ice. Ice
missiles
        burst around us and
                              one larger slab
            could swamp us, flip us, waste
our day.
        The skipper orders us to
paddle fast
            along the farther bank. The looming
glacier snickers as we pass.

And now the river widens,
                          skirts a tidal marsh
with sandhill cranes, snow geese, sea otters,
seals. Three snowy owls
                        stare back.
Astonishing, this gush, this flood of life!
A dozen black-billed
                        trumpeters take off
and mount the air, a honking wedge. Black
        masks and
                  wingtips blur with
                              distance like
the ghost of an armada, vanish into mist.
                              Oh, swans,

what shore will you alight on? asks Kabir. *Why
can't we*
　　　fly together to that wished-for place?

We reach the landing spot
　　　　　　and haul our
rafts on shore, deflate them, heft them into
waiting trucks.
　　　　Tonight we'll shower at
a public pool, tomorrow
　　　　　　loaded in small planes
we'll see it all again, buzzing the
furrowed ice-fields from above, skimming
the glacial lake,
　　　　those dunes,
that shelf of bell-like music, and
the pond we
　　　danced in nude. Our Athabascan
pilot damns the
　　　　　world of moneyed politics and
wonders how this river, sacred to her tribe,
can be preserved. *I hear*
　　　　bells ringing
that no one has shaken.
　　　　　Rain pours down
although the sky is clear. Reason
will always fail you, says Kabir,
but inside love
　　　there flows a river of light.

Then driving home I'll cross paths with
a pair of moose who
　　　　　race beside the car
with blazing eyes. *Friend, listen*, says Kabir,
only the holiness inside
　　　could make those eyes so bright!

167

* * *

A NOTE ON KABIR

The life of the fifteenth century Indian poet Kabir comes to us mainly through legends. It is thought that he was raised a Moslem, though he knew the Hindu traditions as well. Both groups attacked him during his lifetime; however, at his death, Hindu and Moslem mobs are said to have quarreled over his body, debating whether he should be buried according to Moslem practice or cremated as a Hindu. But when the shroud was taken off his corpse, they found only flowers. These were divided between the two communities and each performed its own last rites.

Kabir's poems were composed orally and transmitted orally for a hundred years before they were written down. Translations of his work vary widely in tone and voice (not to mention quality), and I have made some alterations when quoting them.

SOURCES

Bly, Robert, trans., *Kabir: Ecstatic Poems* (Boston, 2004), with an Afterward by John Stratton Hawley

Bly, Robert, trans., *The Kabir Book* (Boston, 1977)

Dharwadker, Vinay, trans., *Kabir: The Weaver's Songs* (New Delhi, 2003)

Hess, Linda and Shukdev Singh, trans., *The Bījak of Kabir* (San Francisco, 1983)

Mehrotra, Arvind Krishna, trans., Songs of Kabir (New York, 2011), with a Preface by Wendy Doniger

For background on the region described in the poem, see:
http://en.wikipedia.org/wiki/Copper_River_(Alaska)

Index of Titles

JOHN MORGAN studied with Robert Lowell at Harvard, where he won the Hatch Prize for Lyric Poetry. At the Iowa Writers' Workshop, he earned his M.F.A. with distinction and was awarded the Academy of American Poets Prize. In 1976, he moved with his family to Fairbanks, Alaska, to direct the creative writing program at the University of Alaska. This is his eighth poetry collection and his poems have appeared in *The New Yorker, Poetry, The American Poetry Review, The New Republic, The Paris Review, The Kenyon Review, The Alaska Quarterly Review, Prairie Schooner*, and many other journals, as well as in more than two dozen anthologies. He has won the Discovery Award of the New York Poetry Center, the Quarterly Review of Literature Poetry Prize, and first prize in the Carolina Quarterly Poetry Contest, among other awards. In addition he earned a scholarship to the Bread Loaf Writers' Conference, a Rasmuson Fellowship, and was a writing fellow at the Fine Arts Work Center in Provincetown. In 2009, he served as the first writer-in-residence at Denali National Park. These days, he and his wife Nancy divide their time between Fairbanks and Bellingham, Washington. For more information, you can visit his website at www.johnmorganpoet.com

salmonpoetry

Cliffs of Moher, County Clare, Ireland

"Publishing the finest Irish and international literature."
Michael D. Higgins, President of Ireland